CLOAK
OF
ILLUSION

CLOAK
OF
ILLUSION

STANISLAW DYGAT

Translated by
David Welsh

THE M.I.T. PRESS
Cambridge, Massachusetts,
and London, England

Originally published in Poland by Państwowy Instytut Wydawniczy
under the title "Disneyland"
English translation Copyright © 1969 by
The Massachusetts Institute of Technology

Set in Fototronic Baskerville (CRT)
Printed and bound in the United States of America by
The Colonial Press, Inc., Clinton, Massachusetts

SBN 262 04029 8 (hardcover)

Library of Congress catalog card number: 75-103895

I was leaning against the track railings and gazing at the green turf. Ksiezak was sitting on a bench beside me. He was playing with the stop watch that hung around his neck and also staring at the green turf.

A silent contest was in progress between us as to who would speak first.

A helicopter clattered above the stadium, pigeons flew by and darted away toward the outline of the Kosciuszko Mound, which was turning blue in the fading light of the spring afternoon. But suddenly they turned back and fluttered in the direction of the gleaming towers of Wawel castle.

Migdalski was running around the track at an easy trot. He'd completed most of his laps. There was an absurd expression of concentration on his face.

"Why's that ass running like that?" I thought.

I didn't despise Migdalski. I knew that within a year he might surpass me. He was hard-working and ambitious. But first of all his running was damn important to him. But at this time I'd have thought the same of anyone who ran in a circle. Everything seemed stupid to me, but this was the stupidest thing of all.

Not far from us Dorota was practicing broad jumps. You could hear the stamping of her feet and her shrill cries. I didn't look in that direction. Generally speaking, I liked to watch her jumping. At this moment it didn't interest me in the least.

"Migdalski!" shouted Ksiezak.

Migdalski stopped with an inquiring smile. Ksiezak began to shout at him for raising his legs too high. He shouted coarsely. Migdalski stared in amazement, because Ksiezak was usually polite toward us.

Migdalski hadn't been lifting his legs too high, and even if he had, what of it? Besides, Ksiezak couldn't have seen him, since he hadn't shifted his gaze from the green turf. I sometimes glanced at Migdalski. Because he got on my nerves. Ksiezak, furious because I didn't want to be the first to speak was taking it out on Migdalski. Then he shouted at him to stop. But after all, he had to in order to find out what Ksiezak wanted. After a brief moment of hesitation, Migdalski started running again. I felt sorry for him. I wasn't all that fond of him, but it was because of me that Ksiezak had shouted at him.

"God damn sad sack," Ksiezak muttered. As though to himself. In fact he was begging me to speak. I said nothing. I was growing increasingly angry with Ksiezak. But when I realized how base that was on my part, I felt nauseated. Still, I couldn't do anything about it.

Dorota came up. She straightened the legs of her shorts. They certainly weren't too tight. She was doing it on purpose.

"Sir," she said, "I have some problems."

Ksiezak glanced at her sternly.

"I'd never have thought it of you," he said.

Dorota often took what was said to her literally, and so it was sometimes difficult to find a common language with her. But she had one virtue: she never took offense. The fellows would make bets and think up the most appalling insults. She accepted them all with a smile. Quite simply, such things as insults didn't exist as far as she was concerned. I liked Dorota. I relaxed in her company.

She gazed at me, then at Ksiezak, and asked:

"What wouldn't you have thought of me?"

Ksiezak sighed.

"What sort of problems do you have?"

"But what did I do? What wouldn't you have thought of me, sir?"

"You didn't do anything," said Ksiezak. "I was just babbling."

"That's not so. You never just babble, sir."

It irritated me that she kept calling him "sir." Everyone spoke to Ksiezak like that. Usually it didn't bother me. But this day even that irritated me.

"I always just babble," he shouted.

Dorota's power of naïveté was omnipotent. Ksiezak let himself be drawn in by it. But he controlled himself quickly:

"Well, go on, what problems do you have?" he asked in a weary voice.

"I must be measuring my paces wrong or something. I can't reach the bar. Or something like that . . ."

"Come on," Ksiezak interrupted.

He took her by the hand. They walked off in the direction of the jump.

I wondered what to do next. It was awkward to walk away. Likewise, to remain.

Migdalski stopped and called:

"Come on, Marek! Take off your sweat suit and run a while. What are you hanging around for?"

This was the best way out of the situation. But so that Migdalski shouldn't think too much of himself, I kept my sweat suit on.

I played the fool as I ran. I passed him, then let him get ahead, and so on in turn. He got mad and impatient, since he wanted to run his five thousand paces quietly and steadily. This was precisely why I did it. After I had passed him again and again, he called out:

"Hey you, drop back a bit, your ears are blocking my view of the stadium."

"Henryk," I said, "don't try such complicated malice, it's beyond you. You'll get inflammation of the brain."

This wasn't witty, but it was sufficient for Migdalski. He opened his mouth, didn't know what to say, shut it again and, adopting his expression of concentration, ran on.

The truth is, I did have slightly protruding ears. But girls said they suited my face.

My father was a terrible bungler. This had an influence on my life, for he came to the conclusion that it wasn't a good thing to be a bungler and that physical efficiency led to the avoidance of many troubles. He ordered me to practice gymnastics, go in for sports, and learn jiujitsu. When I was seven he wanted to teach me somersaults. Once during this drill I fell on my head with a loud bang, upset the china cupboard and smashed the Sèvres porcelain. It wasn't genuine Sèvres, but an imitation; this had a certain significance in a later stage of this incident.

Such a fall on the head can turn a person stupid once and for all. But I had a devilishly hard head. When I went in for boxing later on, no punch could knock me off my feet. I had a chance of getting somewhere in boxing, but one time during a match between the juniors of Cracow and Danzig, when I was in the ring a Danzig fan shouted:

"Hit big-ears!"

I decided then and there that I wouldn't box any more. I didn't have a complex about my ears. Some people even said that my ears accentuated my masculine personality. But in contrast to Dorota, I took offense easily. Sometimes I took offense not because I felt sore, but because I suspected malicious intent. For the most part this was imaginary, and people were surprised when I went around looking hurt. I didn't have complexes on the topic of my ears. To tell the truth I didn't give up boxing on account of that shout, but because boxing bored me. I told Szymaniak, our trainer, that I was deeply hurt by the boorishness of the public and so had decided to quit the ring. Our conversation on this subject was shamefully stupid. Szymaniak adopted a pathetic tone and kept talking rubbish about the attitude of a sportsman. He was intelligent, but the stupidity of what I said threw him off balance, especially because I kept repeating, "I won't let myself be insulted." I knew it was idiotic but I didn't know how to stop. Sometimes I'd do or say something idiotic, and even though I realized it, I couldn't help it. Finally Szymaniak got furious and shouted, "Then do as you want, and let me have some peace and quiet, for God's sake." I said, "Very well," and started walking away. Then he muttered, "Big-eared fool." I stopped and turned around. I stood still a moment and then said, "I had just decided you were right and was ready to admit it, but since you insult me too, I'm leaving for good." I knew this was mean, and yet that's what I said. It was mean because I guessed he'd muttered "Big-eared fool" out of regret, not malice. But I pretended to take it otherwise. I pretended in order to put the responsibility for my quitting the ring on him.

People are terrible liars. They cheat themselves and others in matters both large and small. Everyone is the opponent of everyone else. Even people close to one another are opponents. Friendship, family affection, love—all are aspects of the battle everyone is waging with everyone else. I sometimes reflected upon life. When I came to conclusions such as these, I was overcome by uneasiness.

The misunderstanding between my father and mother was just like the incident with Szymaniak. I don't claim that my mother was actually waiting for me to fall on my head because of my father. But she was waiting for an opportunity to start a quarrel.

My father was embarrassed. He said:

"Why all this fuss? The porcelain was imitation."

He wanted to make a joke of it. He thought he'd discharge the tension in this way. But my mother used it to her own advantage. She took this joke as a malicious allusion to her maternal feelings. That she was more concerned with the imitation porcelain than with my head. She responded immediately and returned his dig at her with considerable relish. She had a large supply of digs. She shouted, and my father tried to shout back but didn't succeed. My head was roaring more from the shouting than from the fall. I wanted to say something but didn't. Neither he nor she paid any attention to me.

This was during the Occupation. The quarrel continued a long time; darkness fell. Father put the light on but forgot to draw the blinds; a German policeman came in, and he too started shouting. He threatened to shoot us, accepted a glass of vodka, a meat patty which was to have been my supper, and a bribe. On the way out, he behaved humbly. He reminded me of Kwiatkowski, the janitor, on New Year's Day.

The behavior of the German policeman mortified me. It struck me as just as base as my mother's behavior and as pitiful as my father's.

In any case, he succeeded where my father had failed: he cleared the air. After his departure my parents were silent for a long time. Then they began complaining about the Occupation.

Finally they went to bed, and no one so much as put a compress on my head. But my head was not hurting much anyway.

The reconciliation was only feigned. A bigger quarrel broke out the next day. Not about my head but about the remarks concerning the Sèvres porcelain. Not long afterward, mother moved out of the house. She'd been living with a certain doctor for some time. Everybody except my father knew.

She was very beautiful. I don't understand how she came to marry a bungler like my father.

When two people separate and they have a child, this is usually accompanied by a dramatic showdown. No such drama was enacted in our family. My mother left the house and I stayed. That's all. Sometimes she would drop by for something. Then she would quarrel with my father, but differently now. Less agitatedly and without shouting. When I had fallen and there was reason for concern about my head, the quarrel was about the Sèvres porcelain. Now a great deal was said about my fall. This obviously led to the promotion of praiseworthy concern for me as being the cause of the conflict and separation, rather than the other matters, which were embarrassing for both sides.

Every Sunday I went to my mother's for dinner. The doctor turned out to be a nice man. I became quite friendly with him, but my mother tried to make trouble between us. It's odd, but he too was a bungler.

When I started boxing he would come to my matches and run into my father in the auditorium. They pretended not to recognize one another, supported me with cheers, and exchanged impressions. If they met anywhere else, they didn't even greet each other.

My mother didn't like my coming to see her. Those Sunday dinners were obligatory for us both. One Sunday there were only the two of us. The doctor had had to go to Bochnia for some reason. After dinner I stood at the window and looked at the winter landscape of a Cracow street smudged with clammy dusk. All of a sudden my mother was standing beside me. We stood like this in silence, then for no apparent reason she started crying. I thought to myself that surely nothing worse or sillier could happen; but I was mistaken, for after a while she embraced me and drew me to her. I grew motionless, rigid, and hated her. I knew that this gesture had not been caused either by affection or qualms of conscience. Thank God anyway. She certainly had had another misunderstanding with that bungler of hers. Maybe she suspected he hadn't really gone to Bochnia but was cheating on her. She was involuntarily jealous, like all tyrants and egoists. She even made jealous scenes with my father, even though she was totally uninterested in him. Now, at the window, I was playing a chance part for her. She'd have cuddled up to anyone who happened to be standing there.

When something is really bothering people, they try to find comfort in the support of someone else's body. This brings them psychological relief. Not me. In such a case I not only keep away from other people's bodies, but am even bothered by my own. I go off to the bathroom with pleasure, bathe, brush my teeth, shave, and comb my hair. I try to turn my body's attention away from its psychic functions.

Even today my flesh creeps when I recall that scene. I prayed for it to end as quickly as possible. My mother let go of me abruptly. She stopped crying, and an angry grimace appeared on her face. She gave me some money and told me to go to a movie.

I was trapped in a round-up at the theater. They let me go an hour later, but only after I got a heavy blow in the face from a German gendarme, who was very surprised that I didn't fall over; for that he gave me a bar of chocolate. It was English chocolate from an airdrop, with the inscription "Poles, we are on guard." Most exceptionally good.

My mother was interested in me only from the point of view of the ritual necessity of outwardly demonstrating her maternal feelings. My father didn't even trouble to play at any rituals but concerned himself more and more vigorously with my physical education. But I myself mattered to him as little as I did my mother when she cuddled me that time at the window. He made use of my body for his own reckonings with himself.

He was a lawyer. I couldn't understand why people entrusted their problems to him. I never heard of him winning a single case. He blamed the public prosecutor, conspiracies, and said that everyone tried to trip him up. Despite everything, people did entrust their affairs to him, because he had a name. My father's father had been a fine lawyer. He had extricated more than one scoundrel from trouble. He met a shabby end. He was accidentally hit on the head with a jimmy by a gentleman-burglar he had saved from hard labor a year earlier. This gentleman-burglar was a man of high society and led a double life. Thanks to my father's father, they'd never been able to find out anything about him. He was extremely mortified when it turned out that the man he killed with his jimmy when drunk in Zacisz, in the middle of the night, was the lawyer Arens. Then, in court, he kept repeating he would never forgive himself.

My father inherited his father's office, clients, and above all his name. I hate the word grandfather. It's shabby and infantile. As for me, I've never cared whether someone has a name. I've only taken into consideration what a person does and what he's worth. Of all the figures of antiquity, the one I disliked most was Herostratus. I couldn't think of him without irritation. Quite simply I considered him an idiot.

In life, those who have been able to make a name for themselves by artificial operations are the ones who achieve success. They play on the stupidity and laziness of others, on the fact that they don't seek true values but grab what their eyes light on and what comes into their hands. In sport, such things are impossible. As far as I can make out from conversations in the literary and artistic cellar café "Sign of the Rams," where I used to go only when Agnieszka forced me to, the question of a name on the stage, in films, and in art generally is different. An actress plays one part after another, and part after part she has a flop, as they say. But she possesses a certain kind of likeable plumpness, which works powerfully upon directors. This is why they cast her. For the same reasons, her photographs, interviews and the like are seen everywhere. She has a name. For this reason even producers who don't react to her plumpness will give her parts from sheer lack of thought and laziness. If she were an athlete and her plumpness made a thunderous impression on Mr. Avery Brundage, she wouldn't break any world record on that account. She wouldn't even win the district championship. I'm not offended by artistic circles, but am merely stating a fact. It's another matter that these circles got on my nerves. Generally speaking, I was hardly interested in art. Only as much as Agnieszka forced me to be.

Sports bored me. I was no sports fan. Leading experts are rarely enthusiastic about their own profession. I've noticed this. I don't know why it's so. Maybe it's because of the agonies everyone has to go through if he wants to attain noteworthy results. Maybe it's shame. Maybe both. Anyone who's enthusiastic about his profession always appears somewhat suspect to me.

Sports was my profession. Something more even. I had the right to consider myself an outstanding expert. Winning the title of vice champion of Europe allows me to. I'd have been champion even for certain if I hadn't spent the evening before the race sitting up late with dance hostesses in a night club on a very elegant street of the town in which the championships were being held. Goodness knows why I sat there. The hostesses were stupid and affected, and didn't amuse me in the slightest. But the less said about titles, prizes, and other nonsense the better. From this point of view, sports bored me and I wasn't an enthusiast. But it replaced home, family, and childhood. It was my father who made me a sportsman. I didn't feel grateful to him for it. On the contrary. I hadn't the slightest desire to become a sportsman. Sometimes I tried to break away from sports. I never succeeded. It was too strongly linked with my life. Decisions were made without my having any part in them, and without my will. I know that something happened that didn't suit me and had nothing to do with me. I couldn't explain this to anyone. It was too complex. Once I tried to talk to Agnieszka about it. She said, "You try to complicate the very simplest matters. You lack simplicity." She hadn't understood what I meant, which was why she put all the blame on me. I lack simplicity! Who said that? At times I hated Agnieszka.

No, there were no reasons for me to feel grateful to my father. To him I was a sort of race horse. But I didn't give a damn about that. I didn't give a damn what his attitude toward me was. But I couldn't not give a damn for the way my fate was going. Which way should it have gone? If only I could have known! Longings, desires, and passions which I couldn't define wracked me. Sometimes I dreamed of doing something great and heroic. And out of malice toward myself I wanted it to remain unknown to the world and to other people. The opposite of what that idiot Herostratus did.

To me the sport into which I had been forced replaced everything which that coercion had deprived me of. As though a man condemned to hard labor were to find gratification in it for his lost freedom.

No, there were no reasons for me to feel gratitude toward my father just because I somehow became fitted into life through sports. On occasion I treated him with our name. Previously, he had been asked whether he was the son of the celebrated lawyer. Now he was asked whether he was the father of the celebrated athlete. So much for him! This was his last and perhaps his only cause for satisfaction.

When I was twelve, a backward somersault was for me as simple as a walk in the park. My father had taken to drink. He didn't even know what school I was attending. He didn't know whether I went to school at all. When I swam a hundred yards backstroke, he personally timed me. Once he was so drunk that he fell into the water, stopwatch and all. Afterwards he was ashamed to come to the swimming pool; this gave me so much relief that I even began to enjoy swimming. But after a time he declared that swimming is a stupid sport and that I had to learn boxing. He took offense at swimming because he had fallen into the water. Boxing didn't interest me. In fact, nothing interested me particularly. I was an abstractionist and dreamer by nature, someone who ought to have been born a millionaire's son and travel around the world by yacht, admiring sunsets in different parts of the world. However, as my father wasn't a millionaire, it was better that he be a bungler and on that account make a sportsman of me, which allowed me somehow to establish myself in life. So sports neither interested nor attracted me; the only thing that really interested me was the Kosciuszko Mound. Perhaps not so much the mound itself, but what lay behind it. When I used to ask what that was, I would receive impatient replies naming the geographical localities, like Bielany, Skawina, Tyniec, Lanckorona, etc., but it wasn't this I was interested in; just what it was I couldn't explain exactly, so they called me a fool. I liked gazing at the mound, especially at sunset; I liked to picture to myself the worlds hidden behind it in the glow. Worlds different from the world I lived in, full of unknown shapes and colors, but also having the advantage that everything in them must come out to my benefit. If I hadn't become a sportsman, I'd have become a complete idiot, for sure.

It was only thanks to the doctor, my mother's bungler, that I went to school. He took an interest in what I did apart from swimming and performing tricks like the backward somersaults. When he realized that this was all I could do, he registered me at a school. My mother declared he'd done this to humiliate her. A great quarrel broke out. Sometimes Agnieszka used to behave like my mother did then. And I behaved that way with Szymaniak. The doctor proved that cowardly people always lose in the end. He considered that my going to school must be arranged for, but was scared to tell my mother so. He knew my mother would consider it an act of provocation. In his naïveté he supposed that if he presented her with the fait accompli she wouldn't be able to make any scenes. He was an unbelievable bungler. Afterwards he left the room hastily whenever my mother asked me what was going on at school. I answered any old thing. I didn't go to school. They'd thrown me out. The school summoned my father several times but he never went there. He would ask me what they wanted. I'd reply that it was probably in connection with a trip to the Mazovian lakes. He was furious that they wanted to take up his time with such stupidities, and this soothed his conscience. I'd never have gotten through school if it hadn't been for Szymaniak. He found out about everything and asked the principal to take me back. This man had been an umpire in boxing before the war. During my training, Szymaniak checked to see whether I'd done my lessons. If I hadn't, he sent me home. He was the only person who really concerned himself with me. I owe everything to him. I paid him back nicely, no two ways about it. He was wise and understanding, he knew how to talk to boys in a language they understood. He only broke down once. That was when I declared I was leaving the club. My stupidity threw him off his balance. But we soon made up and he continued to look after me. I didn't go back to boxing. But it was he who persuaded me to go in for track. He claimed I had the form of a thoroughbred miler. He'd noticed that from my footwork. I didn't want to run. However, I couldn't get out of it. When I started chalking up wins, I grew a little more enthusiastic. But I wasn't an enthusiast and never became one.

Szymaniak didn't stop concerning himself with my studies. When I matriculated, he advised me to go into architecture. He said, "You have a talent for drawing, but mind you don't go bad. You might become a painter or something of the sort. You'll start to draw faces without noses, or bellies with eyes, and what then? You'll take to drink and stop being a man altogether. If a person has some kind of talent, he must make use of it primarily for practical and useful purposes. You'll go into architecture." I went, though I wasn't interested in architecture. It was the same way with everything. I yielded mindlessly to anything I was forced into. I yielded to the terror of circumstances. I let myself be borne along by the course of events. I lacked neither willpower nor character. But my will and my character operated efficiently within the system of events that was forced upon me and that was acting consistently. They lost their force and value when I wanted to break out of this system.

If anyone had asked me whether I believed in predestination, I'd have replied that maybe something of the sort existed. However, it isn't a supernatural power but the power of a consistent system of events. This power gains impetus when we haven't yet the sense to evaluate it nor the opportunity to withstand it. Is it possible to wrench oneself away from one's predestination? To do so it is necessary to oppose it with one's own consistency, establish one's own truth and repel every attack coming from other people's routine truths.

Szymaniak had such an affectionate attitude toward me that

sometimes I wondered if he was a queer. Up to the very day when he shot himself in the head on account of Lola "Fiat 1100," an appalling slut whom anyone could take home from the "Phoenix" at a price. He'd stolen a pistol from a policeman during a match with the "Guards" team. This policeman was jailed because of it. Szymaniak was a solitary man, filled with unresolved complexes, yearnings he didn't know how to approach. My father, a bungler and intellectual, occupied himself with my physical upbringing. He, a simple and physically powerful man, watched over my spiritual life.

He wasn't a queer, but he had grievances in his relations with women. This whore was the first woman in his life. He was forty-five at the time. When lack of knowledge comes into conflict with a suddenly aroused passion, terrible things are the result.

At first Szymaniak's suicide didn't make the impression on me it should have made. Not until later did persistent memories of him begin to haunt me. But it wasn't his death that tortured me most. He was the first man I'd played dirty. What if he had forgiven me? I watched the treacherous battle everyone fights with everyone else; I spied on human falsity. But at the moment when I played him dirty, I wasn't able to realize that I was the same as the others. I often became aware of this but did not know how to draw back. Despite myself I was drawn blindly to whatever brought me advantage or satisfaction. How I admired Prince Nekhljudov in Tolstoy's *Resurrection.* I used to wonder whether I could ever bring myself to do what he did. It seemed to me that if anything could still redeem my unsuccessful life, it could only be my not remaining a complete brute to the end. I didn't talk about these things with Agnieszka. But the more complicated everything became between us, the more often my thoughts went back to the first dirty trick I had played in my life.

On a man who was more than a father to me. And who shot himself in the head, because in that head yearnings had become confused with ideals.

I fell in love for the first time when I was seventeen. Afterwards I was in love a few more times. Not all these loves were sufficiently attractive to mention them. But each left me with the same feeling of emptiness and uneasiness. That expectations can never be fulfilled and yearnings are guided by illusion. Of shame that my own and other people's words suddenly lose their value.

Suppose someone does exist who is capable of satisfying our longings. Someone whom, sooner or later, we shall meet. Imagine many things that will never come to pass.

I discovered the existence of love at the age of seventeen. Love at that age moves older people, but nobody treats it seriously. They have short memories. Love is one. At seventeen or at forty-seven it leads people to the same state of stupidity. They have short memories. When love ends, a person can't stop marveling that he was so unserious. He derides lovers without considering their age. He has a short memory. He yields to his own illusions easily, but doesn't believe in other people's.

The prettiest girl in the girls' school adjacent to ours was Alina Wagner. I didn't know her personally, but she got on my nerves. She wore her beret cocked. That beret irritated me most of all. She hated me too. Whenever she met me, she put on a haughty look. As I didn't react, she permitted herself more and more pro-vocative acts. Once she stuck out her tongue at me. She did it in a sophisticated way. She immediately turned away to a girl friend, as though she were sticking out her tongue at her. Another day, seeing me from far off, she gave her briefcase to her friend to hold. As we passed, she seized her ears and started pulling them. It was just as provocative as her sticking out her tongue.

On the morning before Women's Day a letter arrived, ad-dressed to our class. It so happened that I was the first to get it. It was an invitation from the girls at the neighboring school:

"Dear schoolmates,

On the occasion of Women's Day we are arranging a small dance. We hope for a large attendance.

In the name of Class X, Public School 135

Alina Wagner.

P.S. This invitation does not put Master Marek Arens under any obligation. We understand he may be afraid lest we tread on his ears while dancing. A.W."

I read this letter to my schoolmates, omitting the postscript, after which I tore it up and threw it away.

The next day, after class, I was standing in the street not far from Public School 135. Some minutes later, Alina came out of the gate. She was walking toward me. She was deep in thought. Only a few steps separated us when she noticed me. She halted and I stood motionless, looking at her. After a moment she started to walk on very fast. She tripped, but quickened her pace still more. I waited a little. Then I ran up to her and kicked her in the backside. She turned around. She'd never expected anything of the sort. She stared in outrage. She began sniffing. She ran on a few more steps and turned around again. She started shouting: "You oaf! You scoundrel! You'll see. My friends will beat you up so that you'll never forget, you!"

After the third "you," she burst into tears. She went on talking and crying, which was very comical. She stood there sobbing for a minute, then rushed off. She ran away thinking, undoubtedly, that I'd kick her again, or hit her. But I considered my revenge carried out. I'd obtained satisfaction and wanted nothing more.

So I don't understand why I started running after her. I didn't catch up to her. When I came too close to her, I slowed down. I wouldn't have known what to do if I'd caught her. Passersby turned and looked at her. Some man tried to stop her. He must have asked whether she needed help. She tore free and ran on.

Sometimes she glanced back. Seeing me running, she sobbed even louder. She tried to quicken her pace, but it was hard for her. She must have been really tired by now. She ran up to Mickiewicz Boulevard, rushed across the street without bothering about the traffic, and disappeared into an alley off Cracow Park. I ran across the street after her and started looking around. I recalled a film about a sex maniac who murdered women. He had been pursuing some woman and he looked around the same way when he lost sight of her. He had a terrifying expression on his face. I was afraid that I looked like him. Everything seemed disgusting to me. The kick, the pursuit, myself.

Alina was sitting on a bench not far away. Her legs were stretched out onto the path, her face hidden in her arms which were crossed on the back of the bench. Her shoulders were shaking. I went up to her. The gravel crackled. She didn't move. I stood over her and began stroking her hair. She wasn't wearing the beret. She was holding it in her clenched fist. Her shoulders began to tremble violently and without looking up she said:

"You cowardly brute. You cannibal. If you only knew how I hate you."

I sat down beside her, and she turned to me and seized my lapels. Then she laid her head on my chest and covered it with my jacket.

I felt I was no longer like the sex murderer of women.

Love was something new in my life. Hitherto I'd only cared about boxing and my studies, because I had to be independent. Now I found myself feeling like a man who, never having had anything to do with money before, had been made director of a bank. Such things happen in our country. But they end as sadly as did my love.

Not much time passed and Alina started going with another boy. His name was Artur Wdowinski; he was the son of a journalist and he believed that this placed upon him the obligation of showing off cultural polish.

I ran into them one day by chance, not far from that same bench in Cracow Park. They were walking along holding hands. Alina saw me first. She let go of Artur's hand and nudged his arm. They slowed down. I stopped, barring their way. I don't know why I did that. I had intended to pass them haughtily; I hadn't foreseen the rage that suddenly overcame me. Alina was looking at me just as she'd looked that time I kicked her. Her lips trembled. His hands were shaking. I decided to punch him in the nose. Only once, and with a feeling of superiority. But I saw in his eyes not only fear but also a determination to fight me. At that time I was the junior middle-weight champion of Poland. His desperate determination aroused my respect. I spat at his feet and walked away. I could hear Alina's tearful voice:

"He's a terrible boor. Come on, Artur. You don't even know what a boor he is."

I wondered whether I should go back and knock the beret off her head. But I'd already lost interest in the whole business.

I developed a complex on account of the beret. Afterwards, whenever I saw a schoolgirl with her beret cocked, I was tempted to knock it off her head.

Artur was an enterprising boy. He got from Alina that which, in light of the majesty of first love, seemed sacrilege to me. But once he'd gotten it, he dropped her.

I met him often later on. He became a theatrical producer. He was making a name for himself. People talked and wrote about him. He gave me tickets to the theater. Basically the theater bored me. But I settled various accounts with Agnieszka with these tickets. I rather liked Artur. He was intelligent and malicious.

Once we got to talking over those old matters.

"Listen," I said, "would you have fought me if I'd hit you?"

It sounded so naïve that we both began laughing.

"Are you crazy?" he said. "I was scared to death. If you'd raised a hand, I'd have bolted."

Then he added:

"She loved you, not me. When you left, she started to cry. We were supposed to go to a movie, but she ran home."

It again sounded naïve, and again we started to laugh.

People said that when Artur dropped Alina, she took to drinking. She used to go to the "Phoenix," and behave loosely with anyone who came along. I felt no satisfaction. I was sorry. She'd have avoided that if she hadn't dropped me for Artur.

To tell the truth, it wasn't that way at all—quite the opposite. Alina didn't drop me, I dropped her, and it was on my account that she went to the dogs.

A person pretends that events favor his own intentions. He despises the truth which reality propagates. He is deaf to its obvious arguments if it doesn't say what corresponds to his own interests and doesn't flatter his self-satisfaction. He makes considerable and strenuous efforts to give false appearances to facts. He is eagerly helped in this by his most faithful friend, a short memory.

The facts in the story of my first love are accurate and true. But everything was really quite different.

Love took me by surprise, as a new phenomenon in my life. I couldn't cope with it. I didn't know how to fit it in amidst other matters. With all the enthusiasm of a beginner, I sacrificed everything to love. Nothing but love was of any concern to me. I was impatient to demonstrate my sacrifice and confide my hidden thoughts. This mustn't be allowed. For it is here that bitterness and alienation are born.

On that account two beings brought close by love cannot become identical. The identicalness of two beings is the crazy invention of women who occupy their minds with literature. By sacrificing everything and confessing everything the pretense of identity is achieved but this cancels the right to individual reactions to the same emotional states.

I loved Alina, and she gave me no reasons to believe that she didn't love me. But uneasiness increased within me day by day. I considered that Alina didn't respond to me with what my love deserved. She preserved her individuality while I was losing mine, and that inclined me to rebel. I felt I was being used. I trusted her feelings less and less, while my own began to change into dislike. I believed in her love only when mine had weakened. Then I was overcome with horror. Not because my love was ending, but because hers still endured. Resentment at insufficiency changed into resentment at excess. I longed for independence. I was exhausted. I wanted to be myself again. In the end, that was all I wanted. Morally, I am responsible for the incident with Artur. I wanted to be rid of Alina. When I succeeded, I started deceiving myself. I regarded myself as rejected and very badly used. And then, putting the events in order in my memory, I selected only those that agreed with my false opinions. I almost punched the nose of Artur whom—without his knowing—I'd chosen as an ally.

When Alina ostensibly went to the dogs, I managed to believe in my own lies entirely and could deplore her decline with a clean conscience.

However, Alina didn't go to the dogs. I met her many years later. She looked charming. Prettier than ever. We went to the "Warsaw Girls" for coffee.

"I'm glad to see you," she said. "I rarely meet old friends. I've buried myself in Nowa Huta. You haven't changed."

She'd gone through a bad stretch, but mostly it was people who had gossiped. She had gotten a degree in chemistry, but wasn't working at the moment. She'd married an engineer from Nowa Huta and had two children.

"I'd like you to meet Karol. He's crazy about sports. He adores you. He went so wild at that soccer meet with England, when you slaughtered the British that I was so embarrassed. Except that everyone went wild. I did too. But nobody was as wild as Karol."

"He must be a real bungler," I thought to myself.

"When I told him you were an old friend, he begged me to bring you home. Come with me. You'll see what a great guy he is."

"Surely not such a gloomy boor and brute as me," I said.

Alina smiled. I ought not to have said that. I'd committed an indiscretion of time and space. She patted my cheek and laughed aloud. I turned gloomy. My feelings, which formerly had been the only important thing, today merely had an informational value.

Once I had told Alina that she was my first and last love. The echo of these words wandered around the darkened café. They were empty, dull, imperceptible.

I've told more than one woman that she was my first and last love. I was always speaking the truth. When a person is living through a love affair, it eliminates past and future loves.

This meeting after so many years didn't shock me. It simply made me aware that there exists a taste of first love, which cannot be rediscovered.

Once my mother's sister brought me some candies. They had the most wonderful flavor I ever experienced. I got to eat only one. On the same day my mother's brother, who had come to visit us, was leaving. My mother gave him my candies for the journey. I've never come across anything like them. Maybe they were perfectly ordinary candies, which I've eaten more than once since that time.

I would gladly have gone to Alina's to meet her husband.

"You were seen in the "Warsaw Girls" with quite a chick," said Agnieszka a few days later.

"Oh, some girl. A schoolmate. She was in love with Artur Wdowinski."

Agnieszka laughed.

"Oh, come on. I'm not interested in her biography. You're making a big thing of it, as though I'd made a scene."

"I'm making a big thing of it?"

"Well, who else?"

I never did visit Alina and her husband.

One evening in January I went out for a walk with no particular aim in mind. Walks without any particular aim can be dangerous. At the AB intersection I met Artur. He too had come out
for a walk with no particular aim. We went to "Wierzynek" for
supper. We had something to drink and grew merry. When they
closed the place we didn't feel like going home, so Artur suggested
going to the "Phoenix." It wasn't proper for me to appear in either the "Phoenix" or the "Bohème." Particularly after having
taken vodka. Ksiezak had already preached morality at me once
before on this account. I didn't give a damn about appearances.
Not I personally. But an evening in a night club was not worth
the hopeless boredom that overcame me whenever Ksiezak
started preaching morality. Artur remembered that a costume
ball was being held that evening at the Fine Arts Academy. We
decided to go there. We stopped at Artur's along the way and
drank a small bottle of whiskey he'd obtained from the German
producer of the "Ensemble Theater." Artur was really soused. At
the Fine Arts Academy he immediately grabbed a girl dressed as
President Eisenhower and disappeared with her. She was
wrapped in a map of the U.S.A. and had her hair done like the
Statue of Liberty. She had a card pinned into her hair with the
inscription "I am President Eisenhower." I wandered around
alone. I didn't feel like going home, and I didn't feel like staying
there. I wasn't drunk. I never got drunk. In any case, not like
other men. I had a fiendishly strong head. I didn't know anyone
at this ball. I didn't notice a single interesting girl. Couples were
embracing in corners. A fat, bald character was playing a medley
of gypsy melodies on a piano, and crying. Altogether it was boring. I decided to leave. A girl in Oriental costume was standing in
the hall. Her face was veiled; only her eyes were visible. She was
standing in front of a mirror and eyeing herself. As I walked by,
she turned her head and glanced at me. In all my life I'd never
seen such black, huge eyes. I said:
"Good evening, or properly speaking, good morning."
"Good night, or properly speaking, goodbye," she replied, and
turned back to the mirror.
I went over, embraced her and tried to kiss her. I'm not partic-

ularly aggressive with girls. But in the middle of the night, after drinking, everything seems simple, easy, and pleasant. Anyway, I didn't count on success, but rather expected she'd start shouting or would slap my face. I wouldn't have minded at all. There would have been a scene, and at least I wouldn't have gone home with the feeling that nothing had happened during the night. It wasn't easy to kiss her. Her entire face was closely veiled. What was I to kiss? Only her eyes remained. I decided to kiss her eyes, but she bent her head.

"You set about things briskly," she said.

"You misunderstand my gesture. I'm a scientist and wanted to find out from close up whether what's glittering and twinkling here are stars or exotic butterflies."

"I am not a scientist, but I know that what's standing in front of me is an ass. Please move aside and don't block the mirror."

I moved away. She gazed at herself with interest. It looked as though she had entirely forgotten my presence.

"Could you take off your veil for a moment and show your face?"

"No."

"What difference does it make to you?"

"Maybe I'm ugly and only have fine eyes."

"Certainly not."

"So maybe I'm not ugly, but you won't like me."

"Does it make any difference to you whether I like you or not?"

"It's a question of life and death for me."

"What's your first name?"

"Jowita. And yours?"

I didn't reply. Uttering my own name aloud always struck me as childish and naïve.

"Well?"

"I'm not going to tell you. You're hiding your face, I'm hiding my name."

"Very well. I'm going to call you Rodrigo. Rodrigo, marry me."

"Gladly."

She turned away from the mirror. She took me by the hand and led me toward a large window. We sat down on the sill. Two black lamps started moving over my face, as though she were seeking something there. I felt as though ants were creeping up my spine. Surely Romeo must have felt something of the sort when he saw Juliet for the first time.

"Rodrigo! Vow you will never leave me."

"I do, Juliet . . . I meant to say Jowita."

"Juliet? Who might that Juliet be?"

"Well, Juliet . . . Juliet . . . I forget the name. Begins with a C."

"In any case, that means there's someone in your life. You're deceiving me!"

"No, no! It's all over with Juliet. Since I saw you, all the beauties of the world are worth no more than milkmaids, as far as I'm concerned."

"Oh, in times like these you ought not to despise milkmaids."

"Well, as much as plain cows."

"Cows all the more."

"Milk pails, then."

"Really?"

"I swear it on the stars of your eyes."

Jowita raised her head and started swinging her legs.

"Frightfully boring at this dance," she said, "isn't it?"

"Not any more."

"It is for me. You're not amusing, Rodrigo. Be amusing."

I embraced her and pressed her to me. She neither defended herself nor surrendered. She kept swinging her legs.

"Does it seem to you that what you're doing now is amusing?"

"Tell me, Jowita, did anyone ever beat you up?"

"Generally speaking, people don't beat me. Do you want to beat me?"

"Yes. Very much. And I will, unless you tell me you love me."

"I don't love you, Rodrigo. I feel respect and attachment toward you. But that isn't love."

"Lie, but tell me you love me."

"I wouldn't dream of it. Hit me."

I let her go.

"Be off and get dressed like a human being, and we'll go."

"Where to?"

"My place. It's more amusing there. And I'm more amusing at my own place."

"Rodrigo, what are you wheedling me into?"

"Nothing wrong. You'll make breakfast for me, then we'll look out of the window. You can see the Koszciuszko Mound from my window."

"I won't come. You were supposed to beat me."

"Don't let's waste time. I want breakfast and then I want to look at the mound with you."

"There's isn't going to be any breakfast. You're supposed to hit me."

"I'll beat you at home."

"I want it here."

I grabbed her again and squeezed her. I squeezed her so hard that she started to squeal and struggle.

"That's enough. Let me go, you brute."

"Women often call me a brute. I don't know what that is."

"You'd like to be one. You pretend you're a brute and you do it clumsily. You've made a fool of yourself in my eyes. I don't love you any more."

"Anyway you said it."

"I said I don't love you."

"But you did."

"That was long ago. Then Juliet came between us."

"Nothing united me with Juliet. Someone invented that nonsense. There never was any Juliet anyway."

Jowita threw her arms around my neck and laid her head on my shoulder.

"Oh Rodrigo! I feel I might have been happy with you."

"I'm happy with you."

I said this sincerely. And immediately was alarmed by the tone of this sincerity. I was alarmed lest I'd slipped into conventionality and would wreck everything. So I quickly added:

"Unfortunately happiness isn't our lot. I have a wife and four children. My wife's father is head of a department in a certain Ministry and he'd finish us off if he found out I wanted to cast off his daughter."

Jowita jumped off the sill.

"Let's go," she said. "Let's get away from here."

"Where will we go?"

"It doesn't matter. To eat breakfast. We can go to your place or a milk bar. Best of all, let's go to my place. You can see the Kosciuszko Mound from my window too."

"Well, let's go then."

"And there's an extra attraction. I live with a girl friend. She makes an even better breakfast than I."

"But what shall I get for breakfast?"

I was of course disappointed by this girl friend. But I didn't show it. I saw she was watching how I'd react.

"As you wish. I'll hurry and change. Wait for me at the gate."

She ran down the hall. She disappeared in the darkness. She disappeared like the most beautiful dream. I know that such a description is banal. But circumstances rehabilitate the utmost banalities. Nor was I really so mortified by that girl friend. It was a matter of relative indifference to me where I was and in what company. As long as I was with her.

At the gate I waited a long time. Two hours. Maybe longer. Hilarious merrymakers emerged. They laughed and shouted. With my gloomy and disappointed expression I must have looked intriguing, for girls smiled at me and even tried to accost me.

It was bright daylight. I dragged myself home. Obviously she'd fled by some rear exit. She'd made a fool of me.

I awoke at noon. For a while I wondered whether what had happened the previous evening had been a dream. I grabbed the phone. I dialed Artur's number. He replied in a sleepy voice.

"Did I wake you?"

"Sort of. It doesn't matter."

"I'm sorry. How about the President?"

"The President? Oh, the President. The President's in the kitchen, making breakfast."

"Breakfast? You're lucky all right."

"Come on over, we'll eat breakfast together."

"No. That isn't the point. Artur, I have an important matter to talk over with you."

He must have dropped off to sleep, as he didn't answer.

"Artur!" I shouted.

"What's happened? Oh, it's you. I dropped off for a moment. You know what, I'm going to marry him."

"Whom?"

"The President."

"Impossible."

"What d'you mean, impossible? It's possible. Coming, dear, coming. I'm talking to a friend . . . Well? Did you have a good time last night?"

"I've a request to make of you."

"Well?"

"Very important."

"Well, speak up."

"Does the President attend the Academy?"

"Just a moment."

He put the telephone down.

"Yes," he said after a while, "she says she's in her third year."

"Artur. I implore you. Ask her who the girl dressed up as a Turk was yesterday?"

"As a Turk?"

"A Turk, a Muslem, or something. In any case, in some Oriental dress so that only her eyes could be seen."

"Aha. You wanted to see more and didn't make it. Wait a minute."

He put the phone down again.

"She says that she was tight when she got there, and then had some more to drink. She doesn't remember who was dressed as who. If you want, she'll find out tomorrow."

"I implore her to!"

"Take it easy. I'll call you tomorrow."

"I apologize again for waking you."

"It's all right. I had to get up anyway. Till tomorrow. Goodnight."

Next day I didn't go to work. I called and said I had flu with complications. I didn't want to leave the house until Artur called. I was afraid he wouldn't telephone at all. When he'd slept it off, he'd only think of getting rid of the President. By five, I'd lost hope. At ten after five the phone rang.

"Marek! The President found your Arab."

"No!"

"You'll find out right away. She made an appointment with her at six in the café in Francuska. Her name is Mika. So come along."

He put down the phone. I walked nervously around the room and wondered whether it was possible that I'd been such a complete fool. After fifteen minutes' talk to fall desperately in love with a girl whose face I didn't even know and who was called Mika. But that's how it was. I took a bath, shaved, and smeared my hair with Yardley's brilliantine. Dorota had given it to me. She got it from an Italian discus thrower who was in love with her. He absolutely had to give her something, but he'd already distributed all his ladies' things. I already had my raincoat on when the phone rang again. I was afraid it was my father and decided not to answer. But I did. It might have been Artur with some new information. But it was my father. Drunk, of course. He kept on repeating that I was his most beloved son, as though he had others. I knew he would want a hundred zloty. I told him I'd leave a hundred zloty for him with the janitor, and put the receiver down. Complete disintegration of a bourgeois family.

I caught sight of Artur and the President from the cloakroom. The girl sitting with them had her back turned. I deliberately took my coat off slowly. I walked in carelessly and tripped on the turned-up corner of the carpet. But she didn't see that.

"Oh, Marek. What are you doing here?" cried Artur and winked at me.

The girl turned around. She had thin blond hair, a pallid skin and small, pale blue eyes. It seemed to me that both Artur and the President were embarrassed. They concealed it by hilarity. Obviously this wasn't Jowita. I hadn't seen Jowita's face but there could be no mistake about her eyes. Furthermore, this girl lisped badly. She talked a lot, but everything she said was stupid and unimportant. It was difficult to grasp what she meant. She started talking about a large dog that kept barking in her neighbors' apartment. A midwife lived on the floor below, who hated children, and there were angry scenes on that account. I thought she'd made a slip of the tongue, and that the midwife hated dogs. I mentioned this to her. She confirmed that the midwife hated children and she seemed offended by my interruption. Then she talked about the dogs, children, and the midwife. It was all incomprehensible. I drew Artur aside. Artur tried not to look me in the eye.

"Artur," I said, "this is a tragic mistake."

He sighed with relief: "I suspected there must be something wrong, but I didn't want to hurt your feelings."

"The President slipped up."

"No, she didn't. She was wearing exactly the Oriental costume you described. Maybe you. . . . No. That's impossible."

"Do you think that after that much liquor I lost my discernment? No, my dear man. The other girl had superb black eyes."

"You know . . . After half a liter of vodka, various eyes appear."

"Yes. But that voice. And this chattering."

"You're right. This can't be a mistake even after a liter."

"Artur, there were two girls in similar costumes."

"Obviously! The President picked on this one. I'll tell her to find the other tomorrow. I'm marrying her, you know? The wedding is next month."

Every once in a while Artur promised to marry some girl or other. He believed he'd really do it. Sometimes he stuck to this intention for two weeks or even more.

"Artur, how can I repay you?"

"It's nothing. When you go past the Church of St. Mary drop in some time and say a prayer for me. Meanwhile, be off. I understand you can't stand that gloomy pretender. I'll explain to her that you got a pain all of a sudden. Come now, be off with you, and may you dream all night of the eyes of your Bedouin maiden."

I dreamed of Jowita all night. Two days later Artur called.

"Marek, I'm very sorry. The President has carried out a detailed investigation. No other girl was dressed as a bayadère."

"Impossible."

"Marek, come to terms with the idea that you've been seeing things. No, no, I don't suspect you of making up Mika. But you saw that costume in the distance, it made a powerful impression on you, and you dreamed of Scheherazade that night."

"I swear it was no dream."

"Marek, I urge you to forget this matter and go back to a normal life. Did I tell you I'm marrying the President? As it is, I'm late for rehearsal. Goodbye for now."

It was a mysterious affair. But it wasn't the mystery that intrigued me. I couldn't forget Jowita's eyes. I was suffering. I didn't feel like living.

During the following week, our club arranged a dance to celebrate its fiftieth anniversary. I didn't feel like going but couldn't get out of it. It was dark and boring in the twilit hall. I had one dance with Dorota. She looked charming.

"Dorota, what have you been doing to look so charming?" I asked.

She frowned and was silent a moment.

"I don't know," she said, "you've set me a problem. I never thought about it."

Not everything was clear with Dorota. Sometimes it seemed to me that she was the one who was making fools of us.

Then I danced with Mrs. Ksiezak. Out of politeness to her husband. Helena Ksiezak and I never had anything to say to one another. She was considered very beautiful. Everyone danced with her in turn. Not because of her beauty but out of politeness toward Ksiezak. She realized this and sulked. She'd have preferred to have a good time, not as Mrs. Ksiezak, but as Helena. For want of anything to say, I asked, "Having a good time, Helena?" She frowned and shrugged. The dance ended and I kissed her hand. She gazed into my eyes, suddenly smiled and pulled my hair. She turned away at once and went toward her table. I followed her, wondering what that gesture was supposed to mean. The hilarious Ksiezak was throwing paper snakes.

"Well, Marek? A great time, eh?" he said.

I bowed to Helena. She responded with a conventional nod of the head. She looked sulky, just as she had during the dance. I walked away to the buffet. I kept thinking about Jowita. At the bar there was nothing but yellow lemonade and sweet wine. I had a flat flask of vodka in my pocket. I went into the washroom for a quick one. Other fellows were there. Each was having a quick one from a flask. If they'd served vodka at the bar, nobody would have had drunk more than two or three. None of us is a drunkard. I may have a few drinks more often than the others. I still wondered how to interpret Helena's gesture. We talked about our soccer team. That they'd certainly drop out of the first league. There was some mixup in the Section. Artur Wdowinski, the left back, complained they didn't pay his expenses regularly. He was a carpenter and had nothing to do with the other Artur. Migdalski came in. He never drank, but the antiprohibitionist atmosphere of the men's room fascinated him. He came in with a bottle of lemonade. We threw him out. Everything we did was out of boredom. Even Artur surely talked about his expenses out of boredom. It seems it wasn't true. Someone suggested going to the "Phoenix." It wouldn't look good. And it wouldn't look good to leave the dance so early. In any case, nobody felt like going to the "Phoenix." I took a few more swallows. It made me feel warm and good. I went into the hall. The question of how to interpret Helena's gesture continued to bother me. Suddenly I stopped and struck my forehead. Helena was Jowita. Of course! Sometimes she did completely unexpected things. She had dressed up and gone to the Academy dance without telling anybody. I started to walk quickly toward the Ksiezaks' table. I didn't consider what I would do once I got there. Halfway I stopped. What an ass I was. Helena's eyes were blue. A weight fell from my heart. But why had Helena behaved so strangely after the dance? Quite simply she'd felt sorry. She didn't want me to mistake her bad temper for contempt. A man immediately imagines God knows what. Fortunately Helena wasn't Jowita and her gesture hadn't meant anything in particular. In any case I noticed for the first time that she was really good-looking. Hitherto I'd taken it as only the official version of accepted opinion. I looked around the hall. The decorations were pretty. Harmonious and cosy. Who'd done them? They'd wanted me to do them, but I had wriggled out of it. The incident at the costume ball didn't let me rest. I thought about this and that. Basically I was thinking only of Jowita. The incident at the costume ball. There was some poem, or maybe a piece of music. Maybe it just seemed so to me. In any case it had a suggestive ring. In general I try not to yield to moods. Sometimes it's pleasant to yield to moods. It's a kind of game. A person pretends to himself that he's someone else. Either more cheerful or sadder than he really is. In any case, someone else, and that allows him to take a breather from everyday events. As on a journey. I've noticed that people take advantage of journeys for a game. They're taking a holiday from themselves and they pretend to other travelers, who know nothing about them, that they're someone else. The fact that the others don't know anything about them is a guarantee of the game's success. In the gymnasium-changed-into-a-ballroom I suddenly felt like someone else. I didn't think who. That didn't mean anything. The most important thing was that I didn't feel like myself. What a relief. But the scenario was not ideal. Everyone here knew all about me. Even the strangers brought by club members. The fact that everyone knew me spoiled the game for me. It made it one-sided. I decided to escape tactfully. It was boring and also impossible to feel like someone else. As a last resort I could have some fun with Dorota. With her I was never bored. But a delegate from the Central Committee for Physical Culture had latched on to her and wouldn't move even a step without her. Leon Kozak and some girl were standing at the bar. Leon was a basketball player. He was seven feet tall. I wouldn't have paid any attention to the girl, except that Leon had once snatched a Czech girl ice-skater away from me at Zakopane. She hadn't mattered to me particularly, but now I recalled the incident. Out of boredom, maybe. Leon went round to the other side of the bar. The band started to play a waltz. I didn't like waltzing, but I went up quickly and asked the girl to dance. I was afraid she'd refuse and Leon would see. However, she smiled at me in a friendly way and we started dancing. I didn't look closely at her. I watched what Leon was doing. He walked along with two glasses of wine and an exceedingly pleasant smile on his face. He didn't know what was happening. He was keeping an eye on the wine so as not to spill it. Not until he reached the place where he'd previously been standing with the girl did he raise his head and wonder. He began looking around. He caught sight of us and compressed his lips in anger. I nodded to him. He made an impatient gesture, but he evidently recalled that Czech ice-skater, for he looked unhappy and put the wine glasses on the table. He wasn't especially distinguished for intellect, but I had to admit that he knew what the sporting spirit was.

"Why are you smiling?" asked the girl.

"Me?"

"Well, who else?"

Only now did I glance at her. She was pretty. But the most important thing was that she had dark eyes. Not as big nor as black as Jowita, but large and dark.

"I'm smiling because I'm glad to be dancing with you."

"Fool."

"Me?"

"Well, who else?"

"Why am I a fool?"

"Obviously you were born one."

"You're mad at me for something."

"I certainly am."

"Because I took you away from that beanpole?"

"No. Today I'm mad at the world. I've been mad for several days."

"Why?"

"What's it got to do with you? It's my private affair."

"You were the one who started talking about it."

"No, it was you."

"Me?"

"Well, who else?"

She was pretty, but she was also a complete idiot, for sure. I can't abide idiots, no matter how pretty. But she didn't look like an idiot, and her charm wasn't that of some cute chick. She had chestnut hair, cut short, combed back a little behind the ears; somewhat tousled. On purpose, probably. When she spoke, dimples appeared and disappeared in her cheeks, which gave her an expression of childlike impatience. It wasn't a charm that drew attention to itself, and if it hadn't been for Leon Kozak, I'd have passed her by indifferently. In the long run those stunning beauties aren't worth much and all one's knowledge of them is exhausted along with the first look. The beauty that really counts is the one we must learn to know slowly, and of which we discover something new at every encounter. What I liked most about the girl I was dancing with were her eyes. First of all on account of their resemblance to Jowita's eyes. But there was also a basic difference. Jowita's eyes were deep and concealed things she didn't speak of. This girl's eyes hid nothing. She looked at me unthinkingly and even the nonsense she talked didn't find any reflection in her eyes.

"Why don't you say something?" she asked. "Have I bored you? We can stop dancing if you don't want to go on."

I longed for this. Particularly as it was a waltz.

But they went on playing an unconscionably long time. It was as though it would never end.

"Goodness, no. I'm happy to be dancing with you. I was silent because I kept wondering why you called me a fool."

"Excuse me if I offended you. Why are you so touchy?"

"I'm not touchy. I'm asking out of curiosity. What did you mean?"

"Must I always mean something? I said it for something to say. Who are you?"

Doesn't she know who I am? But that was a sort of attraction.

"I'm an engineer from the Nowa Huta foundries."

"And a sports fan. Aren't you?"

"Goodness, no. Sports don't interest me, in general."

"Then what are you doing here?"

"I'm an amateur paper-cutter. It's a hobby I have. Dr. Plucinski, who's treating me for my liver and who's president of this club, asked me to do the decorations for the dance."

"What's a hobby?"

"How's that? Don't you read 'Cross-section' magazine?"

"Sure I do. Yes, I know. It's a mania, isn't it?"

"Something like that. Do you have any hobbies?"

"I don't know. I collect pictures of movie stars. Is that a hobby?"

"Exactly. A typical hobby. And what do you do apart from that?"

"I'm an athlete."

"What are you saying? How pleased I am. I'm seeing a true sportswoman close up for the first time in my life."

"This place practically swarms with them."

"I only arrived a moment ago. Out of duty. Dr. Plucinski asked me to take a look whether the decorations are all in order. Do you belong to this club?"

"Yes. I pole-vault."

"Really? High?"

"It varies. Sometimes seven meters, sometimes eight."

"Extraordinary."

"Nothing much."

"I'm sure I couldn't even jump five."

"Try it some time. All you have to do is bounce off the ground and fidget in the air with your feet."

"Sure, if one has legs like yours."

"All you do is keep on paying silly compliments. You think I'm about to be taken in. You didn't even have a chance yet to look at my legs."

I didn't know what to reply, and didn't want to. The waltz went on without ending. Dr. Plucinski was dancing not far from us. He was in excellent spirits. He threw confetti at us.

"Watch out, Agnieszka," he called. "Don't be taken in by that Casanova. Arens, must you lead my niece astray? Don't put on such a silly expression, Agnieszka. Is this the first time in your life you've danced with a celebrated athlete?"

"Probably," said Agnieszka under her breath, and she turned her head away.

We went on dancing a longish time in silence.

"What are you thinking so hard about?" Agnieszka finally asked.

"I'm wondering who is really who. I myself don't know any more."

"It's very simple. You're a well-known athlete, and I'm Dr. Plucinski's niece. But you could just as well be an engineer from Nowa Huta, who doesn't know anything about sports, and I an athlete."

"Of course. Don't you think that this entitles us to drink to our eternal friendship?"

"With that horrible sweet wine? No. I deliberately danced with you to avoid drinking wine with that beanpole."

"We'll find something better. If only this accursed waltz would stop."

"So dancing with me is such a burden? You're a fool."

"Me?"

"Well, who else?"

Agnieszka stopped.

"I don't like waltzing either," she said, "let's go and sit down somewhere, or something."

I was wondering where to go with her for a drink. I recalled the storeroom. It was located in a passage leading to the dressing room and showers. Of course it was locked, but Cyprysiak, the manager of the club was standing in a corner of the passage and having a drink out of a flat bottle. He was taken aback to see us. He spilled the vodka and began wiping his chin.

"Mr. Cyprysiak," I said, "let me have the key to the store for a while."

Cyprysiak packed his flask away in his rear pocket. He felt embarrassed because we'd caught him in the act, but pretended it was on account of my request.

"Mr. Marek," he said, "I'm very sorry. You know I'm not allowed to." He leaned toward me: "Do you have to go into the storeroom, Mr. Marek?"

I shrugged.

"You've only one thing in your head," I cried. "I sympathize with your wife. Fortunately this lady doesn't know any Polish. She's a representative of the American Olympics committee. I want to show her all of our club."

I took the risk and said a few words to Agnieszka in English. At a London meeting it had irritated me not to be able to talk with the English and I started to learn English. Agnieszka replied quite fluently. This made an impression on Cyprysiak. Admittedly he didn't believe in the Olympics committee and presumably considered his first suspicion as the correct one. But he believed in the

American girl. The hospitality of Poles toward foreigners knows no limits. He took out the key.

"Only please, Mr. Marek, when this lady's seen all of our equipment, kindly return the key to me right away."

"You may set your mind at rest."

"I can't set my mind too much at rest. With such representatives of the Olympics committee, the devil alone knows!"

We went in. Agnieszka took a jump rope off a shelf and started skipping. She did it with the charm of a little girl playing in the park.

"How do you come to speak English so well?" I asked.

"Get along with you! I'm studying. I'm going to the United States."

"To a meet? To pole-vault?"

"No, I have an uncle there. He's invited me."

"You have a wide selection of uncles."

"He's Dr. Plucinski's brother. He emigrated before the war. He has a trading business in New York."

"We were going to have a drink."

I brought my flask out of my pocket.

"So we were."

She put the jump rope down and leapt onto a trestle. I stood beside her and handed her the bottle. She took a large gulp and didn't even grimace. I liked that.

"For an athlete you don't drink badly."

I also took a swallow. She smiled and struck me lightly on the back with the jump rope.

"Maybe you'll come to the sports field some day and try pole-vaulting?" she asked.

We laughed.

"What put it into your head to pretend you were an athlete?"

"And what put it into yours to pretend you were an engineer from Nowa Huta?"

"I don't know. Out of boredom."

"Me too. All the same you let yourself be tricked."

"Not me! In the first place, I know all the girl athletes in Cracow and then again, even if I don't know them, they know me."

"Let's say that I might have been a complete beginner, whom nobody knows and who doesn't know anybody."

"Let's say. But in the third place, women don't pole-vault."

"Don't they? That's too bad."

"I regret it too. It could be a fine sight. But you let yourself be taken in by that engineer from Nowa Huta with something wrong with his liver and who cuts out colored paper."

"Goodness no! Not for a moment."

"I don't believe you."

"You'll have to. It was I who did the ballroom decorations."

"Hm. . . . But look, we were going to drink to our friendship."

She reached for the bottle. She took a gulp from it, and gave it back to me. I leaned over to kiss her. She gave me her cheek, but I kissed her on the lips. At first lightly, then more and more firmly. She uttered a quiet grunt which signified both approval and protest. She pushed me away lightly and jumped off the trestle. We stood facing and looked at one another. I wanted to kiss her again. I knew she was waiting for it and this time she wouldn't push me away. But suddenly I remembered something:

"So it was you who did the decorations?"

She was startled. She leaned against the trestle and started to fix her hair:

"Yes, it was me. Don't you believe me?"

"Of course I do. In that case, you're a painter?"

"Your ability to associate facts arouses my admiration."

"Did you go to the Cracow Academy?"

"I still do. I'm in my last year. Is it your custom to carry out a personal inquiry with every girl you kiss?"

She was trying not to reveal that she was offended.

"Were you at the last costume ball?"

"No."

"But maybe you know the girl who was there dressed up as a Turk?"

"How should I know who was dressed up as what? I'm not interested in that. But why should it concern you? Just a moment. . . . I know."

"Well?" I waited, full of expectation.

"It was Mika. That idiot always thinks up the stupidest things. And I know why . . ."

"No, not Mika. This has nothing to do with Mika. Maybe you know Jowita?"

Agnieszka bent her head and started laughing.

"Jowita? Certainly I know Jowita. But Jowita doesn't go to the Academy and she isn't a painter."

I realized I was behaving stupidly by asking Agnieszka about another girl at this time.

"You know what," I said more coolly and trying to show that I wasn't too much concerned with the matter, "it's a mysterious story. A little like a Hitchcock film."

Agnieszka laughed still louder.

"Give me another drink," she said.

I handed her the flask.

She took a drink but didn't hand it back to me.

"Now I understand it all. This story isn't at all mysterious. I'll explain it all to you at once."

But Jowita had suddenly stopped interesting me. Everything, apart from Agnieszka, had stopped interesting me.

"Explain it to me later," I said.

I wanted to embrace her, but she pushed me away and said angrily:

"Don't be such a conquering male. You remind me of Curt Jurgens in the film "Satan in Silks." Let's get out of here."

She gave me back the flask and straightened her hair. We left the store room. The somewhat uneasy Cyprysiak was waiting in the hall. He sighed with relief when I handed him the key.

"So Jowita," Agnieszka began, "is a very close friend of mine."

"But she really doesn't interest me."

"Am I saying she does? The mystery interests you. This is really quite funny. I'll explain right away. You see, Mika . . ."

We had just entered the ballroom. Leon Kozak was standing in the door.

"Oh!" cried Agnieszka. "Where did you go off to?"

Leon was surprised, since he of course considered that it was she who got away from him. He didn't reply, but bowed with an enigmatic smile.

"Was it nice to drop a girl in the middle of a party?" In my opinion Agnieszka was going too far. "Fortunately the noble Curt Jurgens took care of me. I'm longing for a glass of the splendid drink you offered me. Will you still drink with me?"

She took him by the arm. As she walked away she turned back to me:

"You're not leaving yet, are you, darling? Shall we meet later?"

Leon nodded to me. I nodded back with dignity. Stupid Leon. If only he knew. How little this childish teasing mattered to me. He looked as though he'd been left in the lurch. It had seemed to him all the time that he was of importance to me, not this girl.

It was all beginning to get mixed up in my head. I myself no longer knew which was more important: Jowita, whom I might find in the end, or Agnieszka. One thing was certain—that Agnieszka's company mattered to me. I'd turned her against me. How was it possible to be so stupid as to ask a girl about another girl while kissing her? Agnieszka stood at the bar with Leon, holding a glass to her lips, as though drinking. Leon was telling her something. She pretended to laugh. I knew all Leon's jokes by heart. They couldn't possibly make Agnieszka laugh. The band started to play rock and roll. Leon put his glass down and bowed to Agnieszka. He danced splendidly. A lot better than I did. I had to admit that.

I went to the mens' room. Not much was left in my flask by this time. There wasn't anybody there. I gulped down the rest and went back to the dance floor. Leon was going crazy. Agnieszka danced splendidly too. He was doing weird things with her. I was afraid he'd grab her and toss her into a basketball hoop. I wasn't jealous of Leon. I wasn't even mad at Agnieszka. I felt generally isolated. And convinced that at this moment the final decision as to my lost chance on all fronts had been made.

Dorota came up to me. She was holding the arm of her delegate from the Central Committee for Physical Culture.

"Why so gloomy?" she asked. "Do you know each other?"

"What a question!" cried the delegate with enthusiasm. "As if I didn't know the pride of our athletics."

I usually was greedy for compliments, but this time the compliment irritated me even more. I wanted to suggest to the delegate that he come to the mens' room with me for a drink. I wanted him to be shocked and to doubt the educational aspect of athletics. But I was afraid he'd make it unpleasant for Dorota. Besides, my flask was already empty. So I merely smiled, with feigned modesty.

"Leon really can dance, can't he?" said Dorota.

I made a face.

"Not badly, for sure. But I don't like exaggeration in anything."

"And who's that piece of ass he's got hold of?"

"For heaven's sake, Dorota, what kind of language is that?"

"What about it? I learned it from you."

The delegate smiled, somewhat embarrassed.

"Maybe you'll come to the bar with us for a drink?" he suggested.

"Thank you very much, but no. I promised Ksiezak I'd join them at their table."

"I know, I know," Dorota threatened me with one finger. "You want to pick up Helena. I'm not in the least surprised. The greatest filly on the sports field."

She said this on purpose, to show off. She felt certain she was impressing the delegate. He was indeed gazing at her with admiration. I don't know whether it was because of this or despite it.

I walked off toward the Ksiezaks' table. In fact I'd decided to dance with Helena. Halfway there I changed my mind. I didn't want to appear next to Leon on the dance floor.

Agnieszka and Leon danced all the dances together in turn. In the intervals they drank wine at the bar. She pretended she was drinking. She didn't look at me once. She didn't seek me out with her eyes to see what was happening to me. She'd forgotten that I existed. I wandered around aimlessly. I even drank two glasses of wine, and it made me feel sick. At five in the morning I decided to leave. I thought that perhaps Jowita in her sultana costume in the cloakroom at the exit, would be standing in front of the mirror. The only person in the cloakroom was the totally soused, fat, bald fellow who'd played gypsy tunes at the Academy of Fine Arts. He was reciting the "Ode to Youth." He'd reached the line "Let me soar above the dead world," but couldn't remember the rest, stamped his feet angrily, and started over from the beginning. How did he manage to squeeze in everywhere?

It was frosty. A light snow was falling. The moon was shining through a thin layer of clouds like a lamp in a window veiled by a curtain. A carriage was driving across the green. Wawel castle, clouded in the light mist and snow, looked like a stagesetting at the opera. I raised the collar of my topcoat and walked slowly toward the public gardens. I was thinking that I had to make a fundamental change in my life. Drop everything that had been up to now and find an area of activity, in which you sacrifice yourself for others and forget yourself once and for all: become a monk or join the Party. In any case, eliminate women from my life. The snow crackled under foot. The cheerful voices of guests leaving the party at the club reached me. Someone was running after me.

"Rodrigo," I suddenly heard a voice cry, "how could you leave your girl behind?"

I stopped. Then I turned abruptly. Agnieszka was standing in front of me. She was smiling like a pampered child who knows she's done wrong and that she'll be forgiven. Her cheeks were pink from the frost. She was wearing a black, short fur jacket and a black fur cap. Only now did I notice that she had a slightly turned-up nose, which I generally don't like. I tried not to show the impression which all this made on me.

"Aha," I said, "so you're Jowita."

She laughed as usual, revealing her teeth.

"No," she said, "I'm not Jowita. Are you mad at me?"

I didn't know whether I was supposed to be angry because she wasn't Jowita or because she'd deserted me the entire evening for Leon. As a precaution, I chose the latter.

"No, darling," I said, with a feeling of independence. "Why should I get mad? The obligations you've entered into toward me are undefined and I doubt whether I'd win the case if I were to take you to court for not keeping your promise of marriage. Anyway, Leon really dances superbly. If I weren't ashamed to, I'd gladly have danced with him myself."

I started walking on. She trotted beside me.

"I don't understand your hysteria. Because I danced a few times with someone else?"

I suddenly realized that this girl and I hardly knew one another, yet we were talking as though we'd been mutually involved a long time.

"Hysteria? Who's hysterical?"

"You are."

"I am?"

"Well, who else? You take offense and disappear because I dance with someone else. I had to dance with him. After all, I left him for you. I had to redeem myself, didn't I? And you leave without saying goodbye and force me to run after you in the frost."

By now I knew it wasn't on Leon's account that she'd asked me if I was angry. But I pretended not to know.

"Then why do you ask whether I'm angry? Obviously you don't feel you're in the right."

"Stop rushing so," she said, furiously. "Can't you see I'm out of breath? Anyway, where are we going?"

I slowed down. She took my arm. I didn't respond. I didn't want to suggest that we go to my place. That would have sounded as if it only had one meaning. I was scared of that.

"After all, we're not going to walk like this in the frost," she said. "Why don't you ask me to your place for breakfast? You invited Jowita."

"Tell me, why are you kidding me? You are Jowita."

She stopped and laughed.

"And you're a dummy. A complete dummy. Look me in the eyes. You must have been absolutely drunk. Jowita's eyes are black as coal. I, I must inform you since you didn't look at them, have brown eyes. You saw only her eyes but even so you didn't remember them very well. She'd be still more disappointed if I were to tell her that."

"Stop teasing me. Tell me what the story is with that Jowita."

I looked into her eyes. They were dark brown. She blinked and smiled rather sadly, as though regretting that they weren't black. We started walking on.

"I keep wanting to tell you about Jowita," she said, impatiently, "but you don't listen, or you interrupt. You seduced a girl, but now you don't even want to hear about her. Just like you men!"

"Please stop making fun of me."

"So you take this story so seriously?"

"You know what, Agnieszka, you're impossible."

"And you're stupid. Sometimes you manage to be comical, but sometimes you entirely lose your sense of humor and you won't let a person make a joke. I'm telling you quite seriously that you made a great impression on Jowita. She was very disappointed that you didn't wait for her."

"I didn't wait? It was she who took off."

"It looks as though you persuade every woman to take off when you're bored. Like with me today."

I sighed and shook my head hopelessly. We were walking toward my house. I live on Slowacki Boulevard. My mother's doctor used to have his office there. He sublet to me as an apartment, and the club arranged to have it allotted to me by the housing office. Agnieszka was taking long steps, trying to keep up with mine. She was walking along with her head bent, deep in thought.

"Were you drunk?" she asked. "Confess."

"Today? Not in the least."

"No, that time at the Academy."

"There? Well, maybe a little. Not too much. Generally speaking, I have a strong head."

"You were drunk. If you can imagine even for a moment that I'm Jowita, that means you were drunk. Didn't you notice that she doesn't speak Polish very well?"

I thought back.

"Maybe not. Is she a foreigner?"

"She's Polish. Her parents emigrated to Australia a few years before the war. She was born there. Really, she speaks Polish very well. But it's hard not to notice that she has a slight foreign accent. You must have been pretty soused if you didn't notice that."

I was thinking, not about Jowita, but about Agnieszka, about the fact that we were walking along together, that we were going toward my apartment, that she was dear to me, that just a few hours before I hadn't even known her or been aware of her existence.

"Never mind about her accent," I said, "if someone meets a person on the edge of night in an Oriental costume and with her face veiled, it's not easy to pay attention to the fact that she has a peculiar accent."

"Are you sorry I'm not Jowita?"

"Stop insisting on this Jowita. What does it matter to you?"

"You started it."

"I did?"

"Who else?"

"Well to a certain extent I did. I wanted to find out something about her. It was a comic story and a rather strange one. But then again, it doesn't matter too much. You made a thing of it and . . ."

"You wanted to find out. But whenever I start talking you don't listen or you don't pay any attention. It's odd."

"Nothing of the sort. She interests you more than she does me."

"She's my best friend. Probably the best friend I ever had."

"In that case I'm beginning to get really interested in her."

"Sometimes you're so stupid that I just want to scream. You talk to me as though you were a fireman paying court to a cook so that she'll warm up a leftover pork chop for him, or something more."

"What do you mean, 'something more?'"

"How should I know? A bottle of beer to go with the chop, or a glass of vodka."

"Your comparisons are really something!"

"Oh, now he's taken offense."

"Not at all! Only I wonder where you get such comparisons from. You must have heard them from your parents. There aren't any such firemen or cooks now. These days, firemen make reports, sit on committees of honor, appear on TV, and take part in discussions on the upbringing of young people; they don't even dream of cooks or pork chops."

"Surely they put out fires too?"

"Only if it proves to be essential."

"And the cooks?"

"What cooks?"

"What are cooks like nowadays?"

"There aren't any. Nowadays there aren't any cooks."

"That's a nice way to talk. If there aren't any cooks, who gets dinner ready?"

"Women who busy themselves with cooking. But they're not cooks. They have nothing in common with the cooks who formerly put aside a pork chop for their fireman and sometimes put money into the Savings Bank. They belong to the Women's League, they get flowers and presents on Women's Day and in general they are as aware of the rights as of the duties of woman in People's Poland. By the way, the word woman doesn't indicate a sex these days, but rather a race or social class, or some sort of tribe, oppressed until recently, who glory both in having been oppressed and in no longer being so, and feel very self-assured on that account and stick their noses in the air, but that usually ends badly."

"What?"

"For these women. Sex is sex and it can't be changed into anything else."

"What drivel. Aren't you ashamed?"

"No. It's all true."

"And apart from that, you can know no more than I about firemen and cooks. You talk as though you were of a different generation."

"I'm at least five years older than you. You're twenty-one, aren't you?"

"Twenty-two."

"Well, four years. A great difference. Because when I was seven, during the Occupation, you were three and you couldn't have known about cooks and firemen. But I did. I even got candies from the cook not to tell that a fireman had visited her and ate our dinners. And she was a genuine cook. The most genuine in the world. Not from the Women's League or Women's Day."

During the Occupation we no longer had a cook, only a cleaning woman who came three times a week, lame, toothless, and worn-out, the sister of a janitor in the Courts who perished in Auschwitz. No fireman would have looked at her, not even for the most magnificent cutlet.

The snow was falling thicker and thicker as we walked along Slowacki Boulevard. I'd worked myself up over the invented truth, but it was a matter of indifference to me whether or not it was invented, as it gave me a feeling of superiority. But the most important thing of all was that thanks to these firemen and cooks

it had been possible to escape from Jowita, that upsetting intruder
who had disturbed the calmness of the beautiful snowy night for
us. Agnieszka tucked her head into the collar of her coat and
frowned slightly. We passed a small house, the roof of which was
covered with a thick layer of snow. There are many such small
houses in Cracow. It's difficult to figure out what they were used
for in the past and what they're used for today. Obviously there
are people who know, but people who know don't have to guess. It
looked like a benevolent individual in a white fur cap. I never saw
a benevolent individual in a white fur cap and maybe nobody
did. So it was all the merrier. Everything around was merry.
White, soft, and fluffy. Even a drunk who passed us with the
words "Greetings, comrades." I felt sleepy, but it was a dreamy
sleepiness, not a snoring one. Everything around seemed a dream.
Only Agnieszka was real and for that reason more alluring than
dreams. We were a few dozen paces from my house. But even that
was too far for me. I wanted to kiss her, and I wanted to do so very
delicately and subtly. It seemed to me that this was the right way
to behave toward her, in view of these snowy and fluffy circumstances and in view of the fact that by profession I am something
in the line of an athlete.

So I halted, took her face in my hands and gazed at her, while
she smiled uncertainly and questioningly, though she knew perfectly well why I was gazing at her that way. I leaned over to kiss
her but she drew back and then suddenly pressed her cheek to
mine, put her arms around my neck and with half-open moist lips
began stroking my cheek, drawing closer to my lips. "Aha, the girl
knows what's what," I thought to myself, and was ashamed for
thinking it. The thought came by itself, without my doing. I
didn't want to be trivial or cynical. I wanted to be elevated and
pure, because I felt that Agnieszka was something new and special in my life, that all this had nothing to do with such matters as
taking a girl home after a party. Our lips were almost touching
when suddenly Agnieszka pushed me away violently and turned
her head.

"No, no," she said, "be off with you. Be off and look for your
Jowita. What do you want of me?"

Then I got mad and no longer thought of being delicate or subtle. I grabbed her and began kissing her violently and brutally,
just like Gregory Peck kissing a haughty Indian maiden in some
film the title of which I forget, but which I was never able to rid
myself of afterwards. Agnieszka was taken aback and wanted to
defend herself, but the ground was slippery and we fell over. We

rolled in the snow, already more angry with one another than erotically aroused, until Agnieszka started laughing and then I let her go and started laughing too. We sat side by side on the sidewalk and laughed, and we laughed more and more until we suddenly stopped laughing and looked at one another seriously. And finally we started kissing in earnest.

I awoke next morning with the conviction that purpose, harmony, and order prevailed in the universe. But when I looked around the room, I realized that I could relate this conviction not only to the abstract concept of the universe, which in this case I identified with the interior of my soul, but also to the interior of my apartment. As a rule an indescribable muddle prevailed in my room. At this moment it might have been supposed that this was the most ambitious display in a contest on the occasion of Cleanliness and Order Month. Quite simply, it was difficult for me to recognize my own room. From the kitchen came the clink of glasses and these delightful sounds for which I had often yearned when waking up alone in the morning.

"Agnieszka!" I called.

"Well?" she replied after a moment.

"What are you doing there? Come in here."

"I'm making breakfast."

"But let's have a look at you just for a moment. At least say good morning to me."

She didn't reply, and I heard only the noise of falling pots or maybe forks or knives, and quiet cursing. I wanted to see her as quickly as possible. I wondered how she looked, because when I love a girl I forget her face if I stop looking at it. This results in yearning, as I try in vain to recreate in detail in my memory her dreamed-of features. And on that yearning the value of their beauty depends, since as they are not inclined to reveal themselves in any convention other than the verifiable dimension of reality. But apart from my impatience to see Agnieszka's face, something else intrigued me. How was she dressed? I have noticed that women, when they get out of someone's bed, greatly enjoy putting on masculine garments, pyjamas, a shirt, jacket and sometimes even shorts, and that they walk about in them with a certain piquant ostentation. As for me, I don't fall for this. It always embarrasses me a little, though after all pyjamas can be bearable, and even likeable, because they are too big and wide and they constrain a woman's movements and lend her an appearance of childlike clumsiness. But all the pieces of my wardrobe lay carefully folded on a chair. Not by me, obviously. Agnieszka must have put them there. Of course, she might have taken a pair of pyjamas or a shirt out of the closet, but I didn't really suspect that of her. Nor could I see the slightest trace of her wardrobe. So she either had on her dance frock, or was walking around in her underwear, which women also like to do very much and which isn't lacking in charm, and anyway is better than putting on men's clothes. I don't know why, but none of this suited Agnieszka as far as I could tell, yet at the same time nothing else was possible, in practical terms. This was why I was curious: on which of these costumes, risky in view of the freshness of the morning, the smell of coffee, and the breakfast-time clink of cutlery, yet unavoidable, had Agnieszka decided? I didn't really know her yet! Suddenly she came into the room, energetic, fresh as the early morning, allied with the normal course of every day. She was dressed as a twenty-year-old girl should be dressed on any ordinary morning. She wore a full tweed skirt, as far as I'm an expert in such things, of a light brown color, checked, a mohair jersey of dark green up to her neck, green stockings, very likely called tights, and dark beige moccasins on her feet. She'd tied on an apron, or rather a hand towel over her skirt; she stood in the door leaning against the doorpost, and wiped her hands on this towel. She looked at me boldly and challengingly, but with concealed uneasiness. So, probably, an animal tamer gazes at a lion newly brought from the jungle to which he is to teach various tricks in striking contradiction to the aspirations of the king of the jungle.

"Darling," I said, "what on earth are you doing?"

"I'm trying to bring a little wholesome organization and order into this house. For heaven's sake, what's going on here? Aren't you ashamed?"

"Every bachelor's apartment is a mess. Only the delicate and at the same time industrious hand of a female is able . . ."

"Don't talk nonsense," Agnieszka interrupted. She'd turned red and was angry. She certainly thought it looked as though she were trying to dominate the house by demonstrating how useful she was. "A mess in someone else's house doesn't concern me and, believe me, I don't have any tendencies of a reformatory and social kind. But wherever I am, I feel compelled to make order around me, because that's my natural instinct. When I leave, you'll be able to turn everything upside down again.

I wanted to say, somewhat trivially: "You'll never leave here," but realized I'd be adding fat to the fire. So I only smiled and said:

"Come here! Come here and sit by me. Even if only for a moment. Say good morning to me at least."

"No," she said, and went back into the kitchen. She was offended because I might possibly have thought something or other.

After a moment the sounds of kitchen utensils and of whistling resounded once more. I don't like women to be whistling in the next room. Agnieszka was whistling "The Bridge on the River Kwai." Never mind what. But it's no good if a woman is whistling in the other room. If she sings, OK. But not if she whistles. That doesn't augur anything good for a man. However, in this case, Agnieszka's behavior merely amused and pleased me. It was entirely different from the behavior of any of the other girls who had come to my place. And I needed something different—I continually needed something different. I think—something different from what surrounded me and from what was my accursed and irrevocable ordinary day.

"Agnieszka!" I called.

She replied with an indefinite muttering. She stopped whistling.

"Agnieszka, will there be any sort of breakfast?"

"There will. Of course there will. With a view of the Kosciuszko Mound."

It was the first time since the previous day, from the moment we fell in the snow, that she had made a reference to Jowita. But I didn't pay attention to it. I mean, I did pay attention, but it didn't seem very important. I reflected, "But that other girl must have babbled out everything to her, with all the tiniest details." And I didn't think any further in this connection.

"It's good that there'll be breakfast," I called. "I'm very hungry."

"Please don't think that," Agnieszka said.

A moment later she repeated:

"Please don't think that."

She started whistling again.

"What am I supposed not to think? Won't there be any breakfast?"

"Yes, there will. I already told you. But don't think that you're going to get it in bed or anything like that."

I hate the idea of eating breakfast in bed. I never yet tried it and assuredly wouldn't be able to swallow anything. But it struck me that it would be tactless to say so and that I ought rather to pretend disappointment.

"That's too bad," I said, "but if you say so."

"I don't say anything. I'm simply not going to give you breakfast in bed."

"Too bad. So I'll put on a robe and come."

"No you don't. Please don't think so."

"What now?"

"Nothing like that. You'll take your bath, shave and dress properly, and only then will you be allowed to sit down to breakfast."

"Must I put my shoes on?"

"What next! Of course."

I jumped out of bed and ran into the bathroom. I turned on the bath water and started shaving.

Generally speaking, girls make a terrible mess in the bathroom. They throw around their disorderly cosmetic implements, little brushes, jars, tubes with the cap off, tweezers, scented little bottles, powder cases with powder scattered around and other nonsense, irritating though not without charm. Even the tidiest ones also make a mess in the bathroom. They demonstrate the victory of feminine elements over masculine elements even in such trivial areas as toilet accessories. They deliberately don't tidy up after themselves in order to veil the masculine landscape in the bathroom with their scattered Max Factors, Rubensteins, or even ordinary Polish products, and in this way they demonstrate their overriding role in it. Only on leaving do they gather it all into their handbags with a few movements and the nonchalance of a tyrant leaving a country he has conquered. There was not the slightest trace of Agnieszka in the bathroom. I might have thought that she hadn't peeped into it at all, if it were at all possible to imagine a woman who, while staying an extended period in some house, didn't peep into the bathroom. I wonder why they keep going there, and what they do, really. When I once asked Dorota this, she replied that I was a complete idiot.

I jumped into the bath. Suddenly I wondered how Jowita would have behaved in the morning, if she'd come to my place that time. Completely differently from the way Agnieszka was behaving, for sure, but also differently from the way other girls would behave, the typical ones. I wanted her to come some time, so I could find out. Out of curiosity. That's what I thought. There really wasn't anything bad in it. And in fact Jowita had ceased to interest me. How could the preposterous illusions of one evening interest me, how could a girl whose face I didn't even know interest me? I loved Agnieszka. On waking up that morning, I realized with complete certainty that I loved Agnieszka, that this was finally the girl I'd been uneasily searching for all my life. But I just thought that about Jowita. After all, nonsensical thoughts which don't put a person under any obligation keep flying through his head. Said aloud, they might seem scandalous, but it's not possible to take any responsibility for them, particularly if they come at a moment when a person is stepping into the bath; a person has the same influence over them as over a radio playing in the apartment next door. In any case, Jowita wouldn't have entered my head at all, if Agnieszka hadn't mentioned breakfast with a view of the Kosciuszko Mound. I began singing "Bridge on the River Kwai." There started a knocking at the door.

"That you, Agnieszka?" I asked.

"Who else might it be? I hope you didn't invite guests this morning."

"Agnieszka, I love you."

"I wanted to ask you to stop singing 'Bridge on the River Kwai.' "

"I said I love you."

"I heard you."

"And what do you say to that?"

"There must be a proper time for everything. Hurry up and bathe. Breakfast's ready."

"Why am I not allowed to sing 'Bridge on the River Kwai'?"

"You're off key. Besides, that song gets on my nerves."

"Yet you yourself were whistling it a moment ago."

"I was?"

"Well!"

"You were hearing things."

For a moment she stood in silence at the door, then added, "You imagine all sorts of things." She walked away from the door. I could hear her footsteps and after a moment, her whistling.

I jumped out of the bath. This daytime Agnieszka was different from the nocturnal Agnieszka. And she herself was dislodging the nocturnal one, since she wanted to run home and dress in normal, everyday clothes. I'd fallen in love with the nocturnal one, but I loved this new, unknown, daytime one just the same. Basically, despite apparent differences, they had a common denominator, which I didn't know how to define more precisely. It was perhaps the simple fact that I loved her. I had serious reasons for supposing that Agnieszka had a difficult and complex character, but I was determined to adapt myself to her and give way to her in everything, if only I could please her. I dressed carefully and smartly, brushed my shoes, and even greased my hair with the Yardley's brilliantine Dorota had given me. I decided to behave with dignity and restraint, as though I'd come to a diplomat's for breakfast. I went into the kitchen, bowed and prepared to ask whether I might sit down to breakfast. But I didn't manage to. Agnieszka, who was standing at the window and looking at the Kosciuszko Mound, suddenly turned around, ran over to me, threw her arms around my neck, and began kissing me. We didn't eat any breakfast. In any case, not right away.

I told Agnieszka that she was my first and last love.

"Have you said that many times to girls?" she asked.

"I have, I don't deny it. Sometimes it seemed to me to be really so, but this time it's something different."

"Did you also tell those other girls that this time it's something different?"

"I don't remember. But no, for sure. And even if . . ."

"For heaven's sake, why have you smeared your hair with that muck? Now my hands are sticky."

"It's Yardley's brilliantine."

"Never mind what it is. I forbid you to use hair cream. Do you hear?"

"Yes. I'll do anything you tell me to."

"Always, or only today?"

"Always. To my dying day."

"Ha ha," said Agnieszka. She didn't laugh, merely said: ha ha.

"Don't you believe me?"

"Of course not. You men all talk the same rubbish."

"But do you love me?"

"Do I look like a girl who lets herself be picked up at a party and brought home for the night?"

"No."

"So don't ask such questions."

"But you haven't told me a single time."

"While you keep saying it suspiciously often. You're not modern."

"Is love not modern?"

"You're not modern."

"What does modernity depend on?"

"I don't know. I mean, I don't know how to express it. But certainly not on having a room furnished like this, hanging such pictures on the wall, and putting such curtains at the window. . . . Well, as for the curtains, they'll do. But if it's important to you that I come again, you must first of all remove that seascape from the wall."

Through the cream-colored curtains with a pattern of colored fruits the bright daylight was shining, sunny after the snowy night. I wondered what time it was. But in order to see, I'd have had to take my arm from under Agnieszka's shoulders, and I didn't feel like doing that.

"I admit you're right. This room is furnished horribly. This is how I took it over, and I haven't yet been able to get myself to furnish it decently. But these are superficial matters, and . . ."

"Superficial matters have a close connection with inner ones. When I woke up here this morning, I didn't feel like myself in this environment. It was good to be with you, and the sight of you sleeping affected me," she stroked my head but at once began wiping her hands with disgust. "Please, go to the bathroom immediately and wash your hair."

I thought she was joking, but she wasn't in the least, she was genuinely mad; she pushed me out of the bed and I really had to go and wash my hair in the bathroom. I don't know why she was so upset about the brilliantine. Everyone knows that Yardley's brilliantine hardly greases the hair at all, and it smells nice. If she'd known anything about me, I might have supposed she was jealous of Dorota. I felt ill-used and resentful. I liked Dorota very much. Maybe I even liked her best of all. But how was it possible to suspect that anything greater than friendship linked her and me? Rubbish. Not until after a while did I realize that Agnieszka didn't even know of Dorota's existence. Be that as it may, I was convinced that she wouldn't be able to like her. It was as though I'd heard: "So you got this brilliantine from Dorota? Obviously!"

I came out of the bathroom with my hair all rumpled. I have dark, thick hair, and when I wash it I look like a Papuan. Agnieszka started laughing.

"To you I'm either funny or disgusting," I said.

"No. When I watched you sleeping you were neither funny nor disgusting, only touching. A sleeping man is childishly helpless. None of his stupid expressions so move a woman as when she sees him asleep. Don't stand there so foolishly in the middle of the room, but come here and put your head on my shoulder, since it isn't greasy any more. So when I woke up beside you, I felt good. But when I looked around the room which, apart from the drawing board, looks like the room of a pretentious manicurist, and when I thought to myself I had to get up and move around in the middle of all this, I felt ill at ease. I'd have had to walk about naked, or in your pyjamas or a shirt, or in last night's dance frock. All this might have been bearable and might even have a sort of charm in a normal interior answering to the aesthetic requirements of the second half of the twentieth century. To walk about naked, in underwear, a man's linen or an evening dress in the room of a nineteenth-century manicurist would be nasty pornography for old, stout, and bald officials. I would have felt disgust for myself and a little for you, and I was afraid you'd feel disgust for me. So do you understand that external matters are closely linked with internal ones? For these reasons I decided to slip away, to rush home, to change into ordinary clothes which would be sufficiently independent not to arouse any associations with this terrible room, and to come back before you woke up. Yes, on the way I bought eggs, butter, coffee, rolls, and ham—not very nice, too fatty, but there wasn't any other. I had ascertained that your pantry was absolutely empty. How can you invite a girl for breakfast without having anything in the pantry? No, no! Don't imagine you'll succeed in giving me back the money. Yes, I bought some jam too. Orange. Please don't think so. I insist on the satisfaction that to my dying day, to tomorrow, or however long we're together, I can reproach you for inviting me to a breakfast I had to pay for myself. I beg of you, chop up and throw away immediately that nightmare of a glass case in which your monstrous prizes stand. Why do they always give athletes objects so entirely devoid of artistry and taste? Please throw out those prizes too. You may keep only the medal for the vice championship of Europe. But all the goblets, crystals, and sculptures must vanish from here. Of course—if you want me to come back. So if you really want that, get up immediately, chop up the glass case, and throw it out of the window."

I knew from previous experience that Agnieszka was a matter-of-fact person and didn't say such things just for the sake of saying them. She said, "Well?" and started pushing me out of bed. But this time I resisted slightly.

"Once a set of imitation Sèvres porcelain stood in that glass case and one day . . ."

"Never mind what happened then. Either it or me. If you don't smash it instantly and throw it out of the window, I'm leaving."

"I don't have an ax, darling," I said. I didn't feel any attachment to the case because it came from my home, for which I also didn't feel any attachment, but I didn't feel like getting up, breaking it up with an ax and throwing the pieces out of the window, which might cause surprise and intervention of the police. I'd already begun to recognize that Agnieszka had a practical mind: "I don't have an ax, and furthermore why destroy thoughtlessly a thing which could be sold. I'll sell it and buy decent furniture."

"Maybe you're right. In that case, throw away only the prizes."

"Through the window?"

"Well, what else?"

"Darling, I really can't throw out these prizes. I know they're ugly, but after all they're the products of my work and efforts. I'll put them away in a box or something, but please don't ask me to throw them out."

Agnieszka started laughing.

"You're funny. You'd chop up that wardrobe, wouldn't you? And throw it out of the window, eh? You'd do that if I insisted?"

"Yes."

She smiled with gratification. I was furious that I'd called those idiotic prizes the products of my work and efforts. I don't know what had made me say it. In Agnieszka's presence I first felt like a conqueror and magnificent, but then again like a half-wit. To draw attention away from all this, I asked without any reason:

"Did you ever play a dirty trick on someone?"

"What do you mean, a dirty trick?"

"Well, something that later makes you feel bad because you did it. A thing you sometimes think about, and it casts a shadow over your life."

"Casts a shadow over my life?"

"I didn't want to express myself in such a literary way. I'm thinking of something one regrets and wishes it hadn't happened."

"Sure. One time I met a fellow at a dance. That same evening, without even knowing him well, I went to bed with him. That's awful, isn't it?"

"Agnieszka, I want to talk seriously."

"I'm serious. I don't mean you. Don't think that. That was a long time ago. And that was the first time. I wanted to die, and I wanted him to die too. In that way I wanted nature to undo what had happened. Later I was sorry for him, because it seemed to me he really loved me. It seemed so to me. He was only pretending, out of delicacy. He was enormously delicate in his feelings, and took great care not to offend me. That delicacy of his made the situation worse. I'm telling you this for no good reason. You won't understand anything about it, because you never were a girl whose virginity was taken away."

I felt bad and somehow responsible for all the men who take away a girl's virginity. Suddenly I pictured to myself that fellow who, on taking a fancy to a girl, puts on that most glowing and colorful air of an enchanted and feeling lover, and then at best he can afford delicacy and attention. And I pictured to myself the girl, whose yearnings and hopes gathered through her years of girlhood for her whole life, and even beyond, become nothing in the course of a few seconds. And I thought that I'd started flirting with Agnieszka at the dance because the dance was boring and because it worked out that way on account of Jowita among other things, and that I'd started to love her so that the evening would be more entertaining, and already I didn't know myself whether this love was genuine or invented, and whether everything that was happening was true or invented. But surely this tenderness that had suddenly pervaded me was genuine. Agnieszka was lying there, somehow resigned and helpless. She turned her head away and it seemed to me she had tears in her eyes. I stroked her hair delicately, and then she suddenly jumped up and bit my hand. It wasn't the sort of bite a woman gives her lover in bed, but the ordinary malicious bite of an infuriated person or an irritated dog. I yelled "Ow!" like someone who's caught his fingers in a door; it must have been ludicrous because Agnieszka started laughing.

"Sorry," she said and kissed the place where a moment before she'd bitten me, "but why do you irritate me?"

"I irritate you?"

"Well, who else? You ask me some stupid questions or other, goodness knows why, which force me to talk of things I don't like to talk about. Does it hurt badly?"

"Of course it hurts. Look, you can see the teeth marks."

"Poor thing. Show me."

I showed her my hand, whereupon she bit it again, just as hard as before, and again I screamed.

"Do you know what that was for?" she asked.

"No. How should I?"

She held my hand and gently drew her lips over the bitten places.

"Because I bit you the first time—because I'm making a fool of myself, saying things I don't want to say, and because I'm behaving in a way I never have before and in which I don't want to behave. Understand?"

"I don't understand at all, but that doesn't matter."

"Do you know when women cry most often?"

"Of course. When they're touched."

"Not at all. It's when they do what they had decided not to do."

"Were you crying a moment ago?"

"I'm certainly not saying I was crying a moment ago. Do you want me to bite you again?"

"If it doesn't make any difference to you, this time I'd prefer a pinch. I like variety."

She pinched me. Not particularly hard, but then again, not in such a way that it didn't hurt at all.

"So, in the end, why did you ask me whether I'd ever played a dirty trick in my life? What did you really want to know?"

"Because I did, and that haunts me."

"Fancy that! Did you murder someone? Or steal? Or rape an under-age girl?"

"Something like that. I showed ingratitude. In a sense I betrayed someone. Someone who had sacrificed a great deal for me."

"Aha. That sounds interesting. Am I to understand that at this very moment you are showing that ingratitude to someone?"

"Don't imagine things. It's a question of an entirely different matter. I was faithless to my guardian. Anyway it was a long time ago, ten years back. I wasn't really brought up by my parents, with whom I have practically no ties up to the present day. I was brought up by the trainer of our club, at the time when I was boxing. He did it unselfishly; the only interest he might have had in it was the hope that I'd grow into a first-class prizefighter. He regarded me as a great talent and I was the object of his warmest ambitions. He centered everything on me. He had a basis for doing so. After all, of the fifty fights I've had, I lost only . . ."

"Are you giving an interview for the 'Sports Review' or spinning psychological considerations? Make up your mind."

"I'm hurt that my successes don't interest you."

"They interest me enormously, but everything at the appropriate time. You're terribly untidy. Just like your room."

"And you're a boring and pedantic formalist. Soulless as well. The fact that I had successes is very important here. But if all this bores you, I can stop."

"Stop taking offense every minute or two. Never in my life have I met anyone as touchy as you. Go on."

For a moment I was silent, as though deciding whether to accept an apology or not, although I knew I would go on talking, that I had to, because I was saying it all for myself, not for her.

"I'm not taking offense, because generally speaking I am incapable of that" (Agnieszka muttered "Aha") "but I can't stand it when you interrupt me for no reason. After all, if I were a bungler, all these things I'm telling you about would be of little importance. If I mention my successes, it isn't to boast, but because it has some basic significance."

"Possibly it has a basic significance, but while you're about it, you also want to boast. It's funny to deny it so violently. After all, it's quite natural and I don't see anything wrong in it."

"Agnieszka, for heaven's sake, do you want to hear what I'm telling you, or do you want to quarrel?"

"Me quarrel? Are you crazy? Please go on. Go on and stop taking offense every moment, because that becomes really boring."

As I kept silent, she cried:

"Go on, damn it, or I'll bite you. And anyway all this really interests me. It interests me a great deal more than you think."

"I've forgotten where I was."

"Before you started quarreling, you were saying you had promise to become a boxer of genius."

"Oh yes. But I felt that it wasn't the right profession for me and I decided to drop boxing. I ought to have told Szymaniak frankly. But I sought evasions."

"And is that your horrible crime? You're shockingly innocent."

"No, I'm not innocent. Surely you're the one who is very innocent and naïve, though maybe you consider yourself as being quite the contrary. You were brought up, I imagine, in relatively normal conditions, that is to say in the home of cultured parents with more or less settled ideas about various areas of life and existence, in the home of parents who loved you and took care to bring you up well and convey their views to you. You proved ungrateful. To be sure, you accepted everything which moral and material advantages brought you, thanks to proper upbringing, but at the same time you adopted a challenging attitude toward the standards that created them. That was devilishly naïve and in a sense even innocent."

Agnieszka rose on her elbow. She wanted to say something but changed her mind and fell back on the pillow again. Only after a pause did she say:

"For a boxer you're quite intelligent."

"If I am, that's not in spite of having been a boxer, but rather because of it. I've forced my way through life with my own fists, literally. The only intelligence worth anything is the one acquired by getting to know life and fighting for life. I don't know anything about the intelligence of writers' wives expounding in cafés."

"Darling, despite all this, I'd sooner have a somewhat lighter conversation. This one is proceeding on too high a level. Taking into consideration the situation in which we are . . ."

"You're not taking me seriously."

"I'm taking you very seriously. So very seriously that I don't want to listen to you expatiating melodramatic truths about life."

"I see. This means that to you I'm a primitive creature, with whom it's only possible to talk about athletics or social gossip."

"There you go again, taking offense."

"I haven't in the least," I said and turned my back on Agnieszka.

She tried to turn me toward her by force, but I resisted. I realized I was being very childish, but I also realized that she liked it, so I continued to resist.

"Darling," she whispered in my ear, "don't be silly. Turn around. After all, this isn't the time for deciding the problems of existence. I like being with you, and at this moment I want to forget everything that hasn't any connection with us. Listen, you're beginning to irritate me, and you'll see . . ."

She hit on my weak spot; she began to tickle me. I'm ticklish in a completely weird way. Tickling disarms me entirely. Wriggling, laughing, and shouting, I couldn't preserve my solemnity or dignity, while Agnieszka, delighted at her discovery, took advantage of it in triumph. Finally I managed to grab her hands and in the course of a second she was changed from a triumphant woman into a penitent one. She gazed at me from under fluttering eyelids, but haughty, concealing feverish attempts to extricate herself from the trap, reminiscent of a boy caught stealing apples. I gazed at her with the awareness of my complete domination, with a contemptuous and all-powerful grimace, while her eyes responded to this grimace with flashes of hatred; it wasn't clear whether this was all serious or a joke, until finally Agnieszka started smiling and I started smiling, and we smiled at each other. Although I was still holding her tight by the hands it was a different kind of hold and there's nothing in the world more beautiful than the smile of reconciled lovers, no matter whether they've been quarreling seriously or in fun.

We ate breakfast at dusk, around five o'clock, dressed from top to toe of course. The Kosciuszko Mound could be seen through the window. Against the background of a sky purple after a frosty, sunny day, it looked as though cut out of black paper. We stood a while at the window in silence, and then Agnieszka said she'd be going; I didn't ask her where or why she wanted to go so soon, and I didn't try to stop her or suggest I'd see her home, because I felt she would ask me not to. We kissed quickly and fleetingly at the door, like people who don't want to prolong a farewell.

After Agnieszka left I stood in the center of the room for a long time and didn't know what to do with myself. The room was still filled with her presence, but after all it was empty. I thought to myself that I was now like a little boy who has lost his mother in the crowd during a gay festival, but at once this comparison struck me as being stupid. I passionately wanted Agnieszka to come back immediately, so that the room wouldn't be empty because of her. But I realized that I didn't know where she lived—I didn't even know her name. I could of course call Dr. Plucinski, but I was afraid of his stupid jokes and hints, and anyway I was ashamed. Finally I realized that even if I did know Agnieszka's address, I wouldn't go to her. I felt that this was precisely how it ought to be, that she'd gone her way while I remained alone and was yearning for her, and that any attempt to change this arrangement might spoil everything between us. But then I didn't want anything between us to be spoiled, since everything was as it should be.

So I went out for a walk with no particular aim and at the AB intersection I met Artur, but I crossed over so that he wouldn't notice me. I was afraid he'd ask me whether I was still looking for my princess out of the *Thousand and One Nights* and whether by chance I'd found her, and I wouldn't know how to reply. Apart from this, I wanted to be by myself. I wanted to be by myself because I was talking with Agnieszka. I don't even know how it started. I'd latched on to this at one point and didn't at all want anyone to interrupt me in this conversation. It was neither mystical nor sentimental. Nothing of the sort. Just the opposite. In particular, this conversation was one-sided and only I said anything, while Agnieszka, of course, didn't answer. Sometimes I imagined some reply or other from her, but to tell the truth I didn't listen nor attach any importance to the replies. No. It wasn't a sentimental conversation. Not in the least. I talked about nothing but myself, and sometimes was even a bit coarse. "And why didn't you let me talk at my place, Agnieszka? Why didn't you want to listen? You behaved strangely and evasively. In the end, I can understand. I'm not as primitive as you think. Oh, that's how it strikes you, for sure. Please don't deny it. You were right in saying that my apartment is awful and that it should be rearranged. I'll even do it. I'll remove the prizes and everything that offends you. But allow me to ask why you're so sensitive as far as the details of my apartment are concerned, and why do you attribute to these details the significance of the most basic matters, while you take the details of my life mockingly and lightly; don't you agree that I, I alone, have the right to assess their importance? Why, Agnieszka?

"I can well understand that you were behaving oddly and evasively. I can understand and don't have to point out at all that this behavior ought to move me and awaken my doubts as to your sincerity. But why does my apartment interest you so much, while my life doesn't interest you at all?

"You didn't *want* to listen to me. Maybe you were afraid that my spiritual interior would prove to be as shabbily old-fashioned as the interior of my apartment. You preferred to cheat yourself. The guy you'd slept with had the right to be a primitive athlete. For a contemporary artist that suits the period. But you couldn't let it appear that this athlete lives by spiritual concepts corresponding to the furniture in his room. You'd never forgive yourself for allowing anyone like that to make use of your body. You're terribly stupid, Agnieszka. You didn't want to listen to me for fear of being drawn into something unintelligent. And the unintelligent is everything that used to be intelligent but that was compromised by your parents. I don't know your parents, and I don't know you either. But I know the whole lot of you. Sometimes they write in magazines about the conflict between the generations. I don't understand much about it, but why should I? As it is, I know what it is. Your parents compromised themselves in respect of various values. You all consider, therefore, that they've been compromised. But the values have been compromised too. They don't want to admit that they themselves have been compromised and they attribute the compromise to you. You all remind me of a drunken group who have been on a spree in a night club and are now quarreling over who's to pay the bill. I don't want to be a part of that, because I didn't drink with you. I'm not boasting. That's how it turned out. My family didn't take me with them on the spree. But thanks to that I don't have to believe that just because they've made fools of themselves in respect to life, that life itself is a joke. And therefore I'm neither angry nor rebellious, nor anything of that sort. And no values have been compromised for me, but at worst I am compromised, and I have to explain that. Did you ever hear of Prince Nekhljudov? Surely you consider what he did as comical, exaggerated, and unfashionable today. But do you know what Szymaniak said when I gave him that book to read? 'An extraordinary guy,' he said. 'With such self-esteem and lasting power, taking into consideration also the distance he chose, he must have been excellent material for a Marathon runner. Too bad he's dead now, and had to be wasted on the old days. Today he'd certainly be a strong point in the Soviet Union's team at the Olympics.' Of course that's complete rubbish to you. But I'm telling you that Szymaniak understood Tolstoy far better than your various learned colleagues in Polish studies and literary clubs. And no matter how naïvely he expressed it, I swear to you that he's contemporary, but you are not. And not all of you, you angry rebels from various clubs, cellars, and unions, who attribute to yourselves the right to rebel without knowing the meaning of the word 'struggle.' And it's he who's a man, though maybe your girls wouldn't want to look at him. They don't know very well what a man looks like; it's increasingly difficult to differentiate between the sexes among you.

"You didn't want to listen to me, Agnieszka. Well, don't! And probably I'm unnecessarily furious at you for, like a painter who paints faces without noses and bellies with eyes, you couldn't understand anything of what I'm trying to say, anyway. For you it's a small, meaningless thing to have betrayed a close friend and to have cheated him in the bargain. But if I should betray and cheat you, would that be a small thing to you? There, you see! Of course, you say that this is another matter. For you, but not for me. Because I, my dear, when I realized I was a scoundrel, acquired a sort of special awareness. More, an aim. The aim of not being a scoundrel. It was then just at that time with Szymaniak. So it can't be trivial, since it decides my whole life. Sometimes I ask myself just why I want to be so goddamn honorable. And I don't know how to answer. Just as I don't know why I fought to the end in the boxing ring when I got a terrible beating and had no chance to win; just as I don't know why, when running against much stronger opponents and dead tired, I would make the last and completely hopeless effort at the finish. Of course this was earlier. Today there aren't any runners significantly stronger than me. But the effort to win is always the same. And also I ask myself the question, what's that to me? That effort and that victory. After all, since I long not to be a scoundrel, all the successes in sports and the fame don't really matter. I've had more than enough of that. But when the struggle starts, then the laws of the struggle also start, and whatever a man may have thought to himself in everyday life is now subordinated to these laws alone. I met a guy with a beard at Artur Wdowinski's. It seems he's a Polonist or something of that sort. He said mankind is perishing. Not necessarily in the catastrophic sense. He said that mankind as it has existed hitherto is perishing, and a mankind of an entirely new and different time will be born. We, young and old, belong to the perishing race and there's no help for it. Of course he expressed it much more intelligently, but that was the gist of it. And through this he explained a certain psychic state of young people and certain manifestations of their attitude toward life. I said that if we, as this type of mankind, are going to perish, then I feel that it's not essential to perish with a beard but that it would be just as good to try and perish with honor. He asked what I meant by that. I said that this perishing mankind can glory in the rehabilitation of the finest and most valiant characteristics it possessed while it lasted. The slogan of devalued chivalric knights mocked in anecdotes and by various pious but hypocritical organizations. Instead of growing a beard against these most beautiful and valiant characteristics and slogans, it would be better to return their real value to them and at least to perish with honor if it is really an irrevocable fact that we're going to perish. But if we don't perish, I for one won't feel cheated as mankind if it turns out that I remained honorable. He retorted that I was stupid and that talking nonsense about honor doesn't stand up to criticism in this day and age. But he changed his mind and immediately added, 'Maybe it isn't so stupid after all.'

"A few days later I met him on the street without his beard, and completely drunk. He threw his arms around me and declared he wanted to perish for his country or, drowning, to save drowning children and he'd always felt the lack of something of the sort, only he was ashamed to admit it. A week later I met him again. He was sober, was letting his beard grow again and pretended not to know me. What am I really telling you all this for? Instead of chattering away on subjects about which we can't reach an understanding anyway, it would be better to settle the matter quickly, compactly, and concretely. So I declare to you, Agnieszka: I can no longer endure the way girls appear and disappear in my life, girls who at first are everything to me and then nothing, to whom at first I say the most holy words and then afterwards the most evasive. I can no longer endure this constant absence of fidelity toward everyone and everything, for it is the absence of fidelity to oneself. So if only you want to, you will be the last girl to whom I say the most holy words, and, no matter what, evasive words will never be spoken after them."

I was quite stupefied after a night without sleep and full of private impressions. Everything I said to Agnieszka loomed over me against the background of the snow-covered streets of Cracow, and at times it almost seemed to me that Agnieszka was walking beside me, running with short steps, as yesterday on the Green, in her short black fur jacket and black fur hat, her cheeks pink with frost. And then I thought to myself, "Why, you idiot, are you saying all this to her? You've found the most wonderful girl in the world and, instead of rejoicing, you tell her meaningless rubbish about yourself and your own unsuccessful life. She's right in not wanting to listen. So let her not listen. It's better for you that she doesn't. So shut your trap and go to bed instead."

I went home. On the way I didn't talk to Agnieszka any longer, but I thought about her. But what I thought had not the slightest connection with what I'd said previously.

I was really sweating. Migdalski had finished training long ago and had left the track. Opposite, Ksiezak was shading his eyes with one hand and looking in my direction. I was wondering what would happen if I ran up to him. Would he speak or wouldn't he? I certainly wouldn't. Besides, I didn't want him to speak. It would soon be five o'clock. At this point I couldn't have gone on quarreling with him or come to an agreement. I slowed my pace. Now I didn't want to and couldn't look him in the eyes. The awareness of my own mean piece of trickery was growing within me to such huge dimensions that it almost gave me satisfaction. Ksiezak was a quiet, well-balanced, and understanding man by nature. Assuredly his anger toward me had already cooled and he wanted to talk with me calmly and sensibly. He'd embrace me and say, "Let's quit this stupidity, Marek, and talk like adults. After all, you know you haven't a better friend than me." But I couldn't stand it. Either I'd fall on his shoulder and weep and admit everything, or I'd hit him. Both reactions would be equally revolting. Cyprysiak came out of the dressing room and began waving to me.

"Mr. Marek," he called, "the phone."

Just in time. I ran across the field. I had the impression Ksiezak was shouting something after me, but I wasn't sure.

I passed Cyprysiak and rushed through the door. He must have been surprised and hurt. Usually I asked him who was calling. Shaking his head and sighing, he said:

"The representative of the American Olympics committee, but she's learned Polish by now."

My not having asked him was an infringement of the rules of the game, and for a few days Cyprysiak would sulk at me. Too bad. I didn't have any time at this moment for foolishness. To dress as quickly as possible and leave without meeting Ksiezak.

"Hello, who's this?"

"It's me. Are you coming to the concert or aren't you?"

"But we agreed to go. What's the matter?"

"You don't have to be impolite. The matter is that you once played a joke on me and didn't come. So I didn't want the tickets to be wasted again."

"I didn't play any joke on you, there was a misunderstanding. You know that better than I do."

"Well, I didn't want there to be another misunderstanding."

Ksiezak walked past the office window. Would he come in here after me or go into the gym? They were to hold some conference at five.

"Hello?" she said.

"Yes. I'm here."

"I thought we'd been cut off. So you're coming? Right?"

"Of course I am, Agnieszka. What time am I to come for you?"

"You don't have to come for me. I have to attend to something beforehand. We'll meet in front of the Philharmonic at a quarter after seven. Be punctual."

"I always am," I said, but Agnieszka had already hung up.

I hurried into the dressing room. I didn't meet Ksiezak on the way. I was afraid he'd be waiting for me in the dressing room. Fortunately he wasn't there either. The conference had undoubtedly started already. Thank God. But to get to Cracow Park by five thirty meant I would have to hurry anyway. I took a quick shower. I didn't wash, only drenched myself in water. How infernally important it was to Agnieszka that I be at the concert with her. Did she think she'd teach me to love music? That music would change and improve me? Or maybe she was just afraid that if she appeared without me, it would arouse comments? God, how stupid it all was! And I was the most stupid. Why had I let myself be condemned to three hours of deadly boredom? Serious music didn't interest me in the least. Not even if someone supposed to be the greatest pianist in the world, of Polish origin, whose name I never can remember, was playing. I wonder who ascertained and how, that he's the greatest pianist in the world? All Cracow was in raptures and crying out his name, which I couldn't remember. But it didn't interest me in the least. But I'd go. I'd go and listen, though I'd prefer to go to a Western. And I'd go not at all because I'm a snob and pretending anything. Because I must. This is how the scheme of my life has arranged itself. It's terrible that schemes of life consist for the most part of uninteresting elements and also of elements that serve no purpose. I didn't dry myself properly, and so had trouble putting my socks on. I got mad at losing time, and thought that if I'd dried my feet properly, it would have been quicker. Nevertheless I kept struggling with my socks. Finally I managed to dress somehow and hurried out. Ostentatiously quickly, just in case I ran into Ksiezak. So that I could shout to him: "I don't have the time now, I'm in a hurry, we'll talk later." A wretched, cowardly flight. Sickening.

Around the corner I ran into Dorota, who was coming out of the women's dressing room. The book she was carrying fell to the ground.

"Madman," said Dorota.

I bent down and picked the book up. I glanced at the title: *Adventures of Peter Pan.* We went toward the gate. Dorota was wearing a light raincoat of a moldy green color. The sun was shining, the sky was clear, and nothing predicted rain.

"Why are you wearing a raincoat in weather like this?"

"Because I choose to," she said.

She'd just bought it, no doubt, and wanted to show it off. It was a quarter after five. I didn't have to hurry so much. I could easily reach the Cracow Park in fifteen minutes. But I wanted to get out of the area of the club as fast as possible.

"What are you rushing for?" said Dorota. "Give me my book back."

When we'd gone through the gate, I slowed down. I handed her the book.

"You also feed yourself on stupid books. Aren't you ashamed to read fairy tales for children?"

"A lot you know about it. It's a very wise book. You know, I jumped 6.3 meters today."

"Oh I don't believe that."

"You don't? Then come with me. We'll go back and you can ask the trainer. He measured it himself."

She started pulling me by the hand toward the club.

"All right, all right. I believe you. Let go of me."

Dorota let go and thought a minute.

"Tell me, why does the trainer pick on me?"

"Pick on you? I don't know anything about that. He never picks on anybody."

"But he does on me. You were a witness yourself. What did he mean about those suspicions?"

"Listen, Dorota. Why are you so appallingly stupid?"

"How should I know?"

"You're only pretending. Admit you're only pretending to be so stupid."

"On my word of honor, I don't pretend anything. So you either don't know or you don't want to tell me why the trainer picks on me?"

I didn't reply. Dorota was silent too.

"But I know," she said after a while. To herself rather than to me.

"Which way are you going?" I asked at the corner of Mickiewicz Street. I was afraid that she wasn't in any hurry and would want me to accompany her.

"Mother is waiting with dinner. But it can wait. I can't stand hurrying."

"But it isn't nice to make your poor old mother wait."

"What poor old mother? My mother's as lively as they come. She's only forty, and she was twenty when I was born. Exactly as old as I am now. Isn't that funny?"

I didn't reply, because I was feverishly thinking how to shake her off.

"Well? Isn't it funny?"

"Yes, it's funny. I'm going to the left. See you."

"Wait. I can come with you. I'm in no hurry."

"But I am. I'm going to walk fast, and you don't like that. You won't be able to keep up with me."

"What's the matter, do you have a screw loose?"

"How many times do I have to ask you not to use vulgar language."

"Is it vulgar to say someone has a screw loose?"

I didn't really know what to reply.

"Well, what's so vulgar about it?"

"I don't know. Never mind. So why do I have a screw loose?"

"As though I couldn't keep up with you. You wouldn't win a hundred-yard race with me."

"I wouldn't? Ha ha."

"For sure you wouldn't. I do it in twelve and six."

"In the first place you don't do it, and in the second place I do a hundred in eleven."

"Hm. When nobody's watching."

"You can ask the trainer."

"He knows a lot, to be sure."

"I'll tell him how you talk about him."

"You can tell him. He can kiss my ass."

"You know, Dorota, sometimes . . ."

"Well, you see? You're going as fast as you can, and I'm keeping up with you easily. Well? And if I want to, I'll even walk ahead of you. There, you see?"

"Dorota, your mother is waiting for you with dinner."

"She's living with an actor. Did you know?"

"That's no reason for making her wait for you with dinner."

"Isn't it funny that she lives with an actor? Recently, when I was at the theater, this actor played a bishop. I thought I'd crack up when I imagined to myself . . ."

"Dorota, for goodness sake!"

"Mother is pretty and looks thirty at most. She's mad at me because on account of me she can't kid anyone about her age. But in general she's nice to me. Very nice. She has large blue eyes, you know? Very pretty, thick blond hair . . ."

"Dorota, take pity on me. After all, I know your mother very well, I'm on familiar terms with her, last week she pulled out one of my teeth, and I ate supper with you the day before yesterday. Well?"

"And you took off terribly early. You were scared of Agnieszka. You'd have had to explain why you stayed so long at the dentist's. And you certainly didn't admit that you stayed at my place for supper. Agnieszka doesn't like me. Why doesn't she like me?"

"You're dreaming."

"I never dream such stupid things. If you know Mother so well, why do you speak of her as an old lady? Obviously you don't know her."

"Oh, Dorota. I said it as a joke."

"There wasn't any way of telling that it was a joke. Why doesn't that Agnieszka like me? And you're frightfully henpecked."

"Dorota, do go home. Maybe your mother wants to go some place."

"Oh for heaven's sake, I'd completely forgotten. Mother is going to the concert."

"You see. You have to hurry."

"But who's playing, and on what?"

"Supposedly the best pianist in the world."

"He can kiss my ass."

"Dorota, see you."

"Just a minute, I'm coming. I'll just go as far as Krupnicza Street with you. I don't know why I want so terribly much to talk today. And there's nobody I like talking to so much as you."

"Aren't you going to the concert with your mother?"

"Are you out of your mind? Me go to a concert at the Philharmonic? That doesn't interest me in the slightest. The most boring thing imaginable. You're going, of course, because Agnieszka tells you to."

"Of course I'm going and everyone ought to go. After all, he's the world's greatest pianist."

"What if he is, when he bores me? If he were five times as good as the best, I still wouldn't go. I wouldn't go to hear any pianist who plays bits and pieces at the Philharmonic. Maybe I'd go to hear Paderewski. Yes, I'd go to Paderewski."

"Paderewski's dead."

"But if he were alive."

"Why would you go to hear Paderewski?"

"I don't know. But I'd have gone to Paderewski. But I won't go to this one. You both go and suffer. I'm going to a movie. I got some tickets."

"From that movie actor who wears glasses and who tried to make you?"

"So what? Yes."

We reached Krupnicza Street.

"See you," said Dorota. "I was going to accompany you this far, and no farther. No matter if you begged me I don't know how much."

"I'll try and bear it like a man. See you, Dorota."

"Bye-bye darling."

She walked away. Pleased with herself, free from inner conflicts, radiating life in a manner so natural, as though radiating life was a thing as obvious as wearing a hat. Alone, uneasiness awoke within me. Dorota's chatter had stifled it. Now it was trying to recoup. It was tearing at me mercilessly. I quickened my pace. Maybe she won't come? Maybe she won't come and I'd find a note at home: "I didn't come, and please let's not make any more appointments. You know as well as I that it doesn't make any sense." I felt ashamed. Even in my thoughts I was a confounded coward. A coward and also an idiot. Because after all in my thoughts at least I might bring myself to settle the matter in a manly and effective way. Let's say, for example, that it was all only a joke. Just a game. I didn't suppose that she was treating it seriously. When I say this, my heart breaks into fragments. She gazes at me in surprise and doesn't believe me. But she will have to believe me. Slowly she begins to realize everything. My cynical grin and bored expression are sufficiently readable. She doesn't know how wonderfully I'm putting on an act. So she turns and walks away without a word. Then an expression of pain and despair appears on my face. This face is calm on the surface. But my mouth is tight. And anyone who can read eyes, would read in them sorrow mixed with despair. A moment of hesitation. Should I rush after her, fall on my knees? Shout, "How could you believe me even for a moment"? No! She must walk away. Let her walk away in despair. Despair will prove salutary, it will quickly change into dislike and contempt. A sort of little male Lady of the Camellias.

God, what an appalling ass I was. Sometimes it seemed quite impossible that I could be as stupid as that. Anyway, it's the influence of the movies to a large extent. Since the movies were invented and began developing, people have lost the remains of freedom and naturalness. Everyone acts a part and everyone tries to dramatize scenes from his life to resemble a film he had particularly liked. I think everyone does this to a greater or lesser degree. Ministers of state, generals, presidents, prominent writers, professors, and scholars. Maybe even the Pope. I reached the park. It was a few minutes after five thirty. I turned down a path toward Czarnowiejska Street. In the distance I could see our bench. It was deserted. At this moment I was seized by a panicky fear that she wasn't coming. A moment earlier I'd been longing for just that. But the sight of the empty bench kindled in me feelings I'd forgotten when I felt certain of meeting her soon. At this moment I longed for nothing as much as I longed for her to come. I sat down on the bench. I sat there by myself and kept thinking that I was sitting there by myself. The gravel began crunching. I raised my eyes. I was waiting. An elderly man and a pretty young girl emerged from a side path. The girl was putting on hideous airs and graces. Her father, or a lover of sour apples? They walked past me, slowly, strolling. I hated them. Because they were so carelessly unaware of the disappointment they'd caused me. The gravel crunched again. After a moment I breathed with relief. She was walking along with a white flower in her hand, smiling at me. I didn't rise from the bench. It's the most marvellous feeling of relief when we finally see the person for whom we've been waiting so very impatiently. I didn't rise. I didn't want to cheapen the price of my joy by a courteous gesture. She didn't even say good evening. She sat down on the bench at a certain distance from me. She stroked the white flower which she was holding in front of her in her left hand. What happiness that the bench wasn't empty.

"Good evening," I said after a moment.

"Good evening," she replied. She still wasn't looking at me. "You were late," she said. "Five whole minutes."

"I'm sorry . . . just a moment, though. You're the one who was late."

"Here you have the best proof that appearances often mislead. Don't trust appearances. I advise you not to trust them. Here."

She gave me the white flower.

"Is it for me?"

I didn't know what to do with it.

"Especially for you. I've already been here before you. Because you were late I went for a stroll. On the way I picked this flower for you. Pretty, isn't it?"

"The prettiest flower I ever saw."

I put it in my buttonhole.

"Do you often get flowers?"

"On the occasion of races or other nonsense."

"Doesn't Agnieszka ever give you flowers?"

"Agnieszka? What an idea. I quarreled with Edward today."

"What about?"

"I don't want to take part in the Memorial race."

"Why?"

"I don't want to, that's all."

I wanted to compete in the Memorial race very much. It was important to me for various reasons. But no matter what Ksiezak would have started to talk about that day, I'd have had to contradict him.

"It means a great deal to Edward. He told me he's put you up for longer distances and there's a chance for you to win the Memorial race."

"Don't you have anything more interesting to talk about at home?"

"We like to talk about you. Anything wrong with that?"

I had the impression I'd offended her. I moved closer and put my hand on hers. Her hand was motionless, as though pondering. Slowly her fingers started to move. They lightly took mine. After a moment she drew her hand away, raised it and started to fix her hair.

The elderly man with the affected girl were coming back. They stopped not far from us and sat down on an opposite bench. They were not father and daughter. Helena glanced at her watch.

"Heavens, how late it is," she said, "I ought to have been home long ago. When we arranged to meet, yesterday, I completely forgot we'd be going to the concert today. I left Edward his dinner and a note that I'm going to the dressmaker. But I still have to change, do my hair, tidy up. What a life."

"Why did you tell the lie that you were going to the dressmaker?"

"Next time I'll tell him I have a date with you."

I made a fool of myself by asking that question.

"You're somehow strange today."

"You're imagining things. Really, I have to run. Are you going to the concert?"

"Yes."

"Does it amuse you?"

"No."

"Me neither. When they play Chopin that's another story. But those other things, God forbid."

"So why are you going?"

"And you?"

"For the same reasons."

Helena rose. How slender and beautiful she was. She gazed at me with her blue eyes. I didn't know whether she was looking at me with dislike, tenderness, or regret. Women's looks rarely have only one meaning.

"Goodbye, darling," said Helena.

I waited for her to add: "I'll call you tomorrow," "When shall we meet?" or something of the sort. She didn't add anything. I decided not to add anything either.

"Goodbye," I said.

Helena smiled. Again I didn't know whether that smile meant regret or contempt. She walked away. I stayed on the bench. To think that only a while ago I'd been fancying various forms of dramatic separation. I'd made a fool of myself. Sometimes it's more unpleasant to make a fool of oneself by oneself than to do so in public. It seems I'd imagined things to myself which didn't exist. This statement caused me relief. A quite strange relief, which I'd as soon not have felt. How had I let myself be taken in by it all?

The old satyr on the opposite bench nudged his girl and began whispering something to her. She glanced at me with interest. I keep forgetting that many people in Cracow know me by sight. I ought not to put on such a stupid expression in a public place. I got up and walked away.

What did Helena want of me, or maybe rather, what had she wanted? And why had I let myself be taken in? Had I let myself be taken in? Properly speaking, nothing had happened. Nothing had happened yet. I ought to go home and change. I was terribly reluctant. Agnieszka would certainly greet me nicely if I turned up at the Philharmonic in a sweater, without jacket and tie. Let her greet me as she wished. It all bored me already. However I did go home. I wasn't scared of Agnieszka. But I needed a hot bath very much.

It's pleasant to lie in hot, snug water. It seems to a man lying in hot water that the stings of fate can't reach him. That he's an independent being, capable of making the most difficult decisions. Sometimes it's happened to me that I've made decisions in the bath which afterwards proved totally unreal. If Helena ever called me again, I was determined to reply, "I'm terribly sorry, but for the next few days I'll be very busy." This time, however, even the bath let me down. I realized at once that it would turn out otherwise. If only she'd called, I'd rush to her immediately. Wherever and whenever she wanted. And yet I'd known Helena so long and hadn't, in general, paid any attention to her.

Two weeks before, Ksiczak had given me an English book about athletics. He asked me to look through it and report to him. I went to him next day, as we'd arranged. Helena opened the door. She was in a robe. An ugly Chinese robe. Not made up and somewhat disheveled, she struck me as being far more intriguing than usual. I used to repeat after other people, thoughtlessly, that Helena Ksiezak is pretty. To tell the truth, I didn't like her at all. But how can one be perfectly sure who pleases and who doesn't?

Seeing me, Helena slapped her forehead:

"Marek! Don't be angry. I completely forgot. Come in. Don't tell Edward, I implore you."

"I'll be happy to carry out your wishes, if I can only find out what it is I'm not to tell him."

"Sit down. Make yourself at home."

Generally she was haughty and sulky. Now she seemed completely at ease. Even that ugly Chinese robe acquired charm. I had the impression that she was someone I was seeing for the first time. She aroused a feeling of good will in me. A new, fresh feeling, one I was not used to.

"Marek, you'll kill me. They called Edward to Warsaw suddenly. He was in so much of a hurry that he didn't even have time to let you know. He asked me to call you. Go on, kill me, I forgot."

"I honestly don't know why you're making a big thing of it. I'm very glad it worked out like this."

Helena looked at me.

"Like what?"

"Rather strangely. Thanks to your not remembering, I now have the pleasure of seeing you."

She continued to gaze at me. She frowned. She was surprised. I'd never spoken to her in this way before. I was surprised myself. Only after a while did Helena smile:

"You're very sweet," she said, with the reserve a person adopts most often when he doesn't trust the durability of a compliment.

She started to straighten her hair and peeped into the mirror. This mirror was very unattractive. In a gold frame, it hung over a birchwood commode, equally unattractive. All women behave alike in face of a compliment. Helena glanced at her robe and suddenly covered herself with both hands, as if she were naked.

"Excuse my receiving you dressed like this," she said, "I thought you were supposed to come later."

A moment earlier she'd declared that she'd forgotten to warn me of Ksiezak's sudden departure. It seemed strange to me but I've known for quite a time that drawing logical conclusions from inconsequential premises doesn't lead anywhere with women.

"I must be going. I apologize for turning up so suddenly."

"You're too polite. This robe is awful. I only wear it when I'm sure that nobody will see me in it. For tidying up, cooking, or other domestic tasks. My mother-in-law gave it to me. She hates me. An old Cracow gossip. Don't leave yet. I know I'm repulsive in this robe. I'll change right away. Wait. We'll have some tea. Somehow I'm not myself today. I'm glad someone's come I can talk to."

She didn't wait for a reply, and went into the other room. It had always seemed to me that Helena didn't like me. I wasn't crazy about her, either. I could take her or leave her.

Sometimes a completely useless object lies on a desk or in a drawer. One day, by accident, its usefulness is revealed. Then we feel as though we'd received a present or won a large sum at cards. I had a similar feeling then about Helena. She came back sooner than might have been expected of a woman who'd gone to change. She wore tight red pants and a black golf sweater. She'd tied her hair up with a blue ribbon. Rays of the late afternoon sun sinking into the west cast beams on the wall. Such beams aren't pink or brick-red. They have some very special color of the rays of the setting sun. Someone in the next apartment was playing Tchaikovsky's *Song of Autumn*. It suited the mood of that afternoon. Even though it was spring.

Helena placed before me tea which I didn't feel like drinking. She smiled. Her lips were slightly colored. Barely touched up with lipstick.

"Why aren't you feeling yourself?" I asked.

She sat down at the table opposite me:

"In general I don't feel myself. Maybe you'd like wine?"

"No thanks. Why don't you feel yourself?"

"I don't know. Life is passing, and so what? I don't get much out of life."

"Oh come on. You're pretty, young . . ."

"Say what you want. Neither pretty nor so young, either. If you intend to comfort me with meaningless compliments, you'd better not say anything. What do you think? I'm thirty-two already. Thirty-two years have passed. In October I'll be thirty-three. I don't intend to hide it. That's not my way. What does one gain by it?"

"You think it's so old?"

"That depends. Compared with my grandmother it isn't. But compared with all of you?"

"Honestly, Helena, it's much too soon for you to develop such complexes."

"Too soon, you think? I think it's high time. In any case, I have other complexes as well. I can display to you an impressive range of them."

"Such as?"

"Such as, for example, the complex that all of you are something, but I'm nothing."

"Sometimes you're high-strung for no reason whatever."

"High-strung without any reason! Better keep silent when you don't know what you're saying. All of you race, jump, paint pictures. And I? I'm nothing and will remain nothing. Ksiezak's wife. That's my only reason for existing. And that's exactly how all of you regard me."

"Don't make up such stories!"

"Don't you make up such stories."

"People admire you. Not only because you're so beautiful. You have an unusual personality. If you were not Edward's wife, it would be exactly the same."

"Don't you try and con me with talk of personality. Everything bores me. And my personality most of all. You can't imagine how nothing happens in my life. Your life is something entirely different. The opposite of mine. In the first place, you don't know the various horrors that torment a person. The worst of them is the fear that comes from the belief that one is wasting one's life. That one won't ever experience anything. Sometimes panic seizes a person. He wants to grab life, at any price. There's even a saying: to get a tight grip on life. You know what? I wanted to become a botanist."

"Why didn't you?"

"On account of Edward. He didn't allow me to study. He has his damn bourgeois theories. He inherited them from his mother. And I had to pay for them. There you are! Before our marriage, he said, 'Since botany interests you, you'll be able to find your satisfaction in making salads for dinner.' That's not very witty, is it?"

"Then why did you marry him?"

"I was young and stupid. I loved him. Besides, I still do. He has various faults, but basically he's very good to me. Now I wouldn't be so stupid any more. It's not worth sacrificing anything for love. Would you sacrifice anything for love?"

"Probably not. But perhaps for something else. For some consistent act, an honorable deed . . ."

"I don't understand."

"Do you understand that a person runs around some damn grass plot and wants to run as fast as possible at any price? To arrive first, before the others?"

"I understand that. Although I myself wouldn't want to run like that. But what's that got to do with it?"

"It's relevant. Life is a sort of goddamn Olympics. A struggle in various competitions is going on in it, but everywhere a person has to hold to certain principles of his own. To force himself to a fiendish effort despite everything, and sometimes even apparently despite common sense. In order to conquer. Sometimes a person wonders what the victory means to him, really. Why renounce so many things for it? But no matter what conclusions he comes to, that it doesn't pay and hasn't any meaning, he throws himself into the fight again next time. Without considering anything else, he strives for victory. Unless he's an absolute, hopeless slob."

Like all women, Helena had the habit of sometimes asking a question without being interested in the reply.

"I've always liked butterflies, beetles, and bees," she said. "I had many different herbariums and up to this day I'm expert on all this. And since you're talking about the Olympics, Edward swears that you'll get a medal. You don't even realize his attitude toward you. He says he'll put all his effort and ambition into you. He declares you're a runner of high quality, only as capricious as a ballet dancer."

I suddenly remembered something I'd completely forgotten. How Helena had tugged at my hair at the dance.

"I don't give a damn about the Olympics," I said, "nor the medals."

"But a moment ago you were telling me that a person must struggle and strive for victory at the cost of the greatest renunciations."

"There's a great deal of difference between a struggle and victory which are private, for oneself alone, and all that circus with judges, organizers, a paying audience, and photographers."

"But I don't believe you. I'm sure it's important to you."

"In a way. From force of habit and the vice of accommodating myself to general customs. But basically I don't give a damn about it all."

"Oh, how I'd like to get a gold medal or something of the sort. You overact. You overact, that's all."

"On my word of honor, I don't. Anyway, do you imagine I never think of the fact that life is running away? And what help is my running, my medals and honors, when life is getting away? I won't catch up with it. I can also tell you that I wanted something entirely different for myself in life. Basically, although our situations in life seem entirely different, I have feelings very much like yours."

"You know what, Marek, that's extraordinary. It seems to me you know perfectly how to understand a woman. I really never expected that. What did you want out of life?"

"I don't exactly know. But something entirely different from what I have. It's possible to acquire Olympic medals, honorable titles and I don't know what else, it's possible to be admired by crowds, and despite that life can seem damnably ordinary and not distinguished by anything . . . Believe me, I promise you."

Helena leaned her head on one hand and gazed at the window, through which nothing could be seen but the shabby walls of the apartment house opposite. We were drinking tea. Rather, I was pretending to drink while Helena wasn't drinking at all.

The Ksiezaks' apartment was furnished in a still more hopelessly bourgeois style than mine before Agnieszka modernized it. In mine there was at least a mess which could bear witness to it all being temporary. Their hopeless, mass-produced furniture from the big stores, carpets, doilies, little tablecloths, glass, porcelain, pictures on the walls, and other details were carefully arranged and ordered. Even primped up. By Helena, of course, who tried to be equal to the position of a professional wife which had been thrust upon her. I didn't understand how it could be that such an interior didn't jar on Ksiezak. Even though, as Helena said, there sometimes crept out of him the Cracow stick-in-the-mud which he'd gotten from his mother. Ksiezak was a cultured man, intelligent, with an open mind. He had a passion for literature and music, which I for one can't say of myself. He was an expert on politics and interested in scientific matters. He'd wanted to be a pianist, and even began attending a conservatory. But somehow it didn't come to anything, so he went into the Academy of Physical Education. He was ten years older than I, but he treated me as a contemporary. He regarded me as something better than other athletes. I don't know why this struck me funny. Various feeble intellectuals are disgusted by sports and are upset because people are more excited by the throwing of a disk several dozen yards than by disputations on the soul. They regard all sportsmen as cavemen, and sports as a manifestation of idiocy and the world turning boorish. If one of them had talked to Ksiezak, he'd have been very surprised. Sure, there are half-wits among athletes too. But don't they also exist among painters, actors, and even writers? I met more than one such through Agnieszka. They paint pictures nobody looks at, act in plays nobody goes to, and write books nobody reads. Sometimes they even get prizes and distinctions. Among us, the likes of these drop out in the preliminaries. And nothing helps. I don't want to offend anyone by calling intellectuals weaklings. But for the most part they really are weaklings. This arouses in me suspicions as to the value of their judgments of the world and people. They're capable of evaluating weakness with accuracy, but they don't know much about strength, which seems to them the vital weapon of boors and brutes. People often despise what's valuable but what they themselves don't possess. I consider that all these intellectuals, missionaries, and noble idealists who love the good and beautiful would be a pushover for boors and brutes. All this is quite unnecessary. Instead of struggling against force, by leaning on strength, they lean on their own weakness. They claim this weakness is an elevated, precious, and disarming value. If some intellectual hit a hooligan who set upon him, he could then afterwards write a moralizing article to the effect that one must be good, noble, and respectable. I think that this hooligan, reading such an article in the hospital, would reflect somewhat critically on his own life. But if he hit the intellectual, and then read the latter's tearful considerations on the subject of hooliganism, he'd only regret that he hadn't given him a few kicks in token of farewell. I don't know whether it's true, but Artur Wdowinski states that the Greek tragedians, like Sophocles and the others, were excellent athletes and well made physically. This would explain the fact that their work has lasted for centuries and is relevant to this day. They didn't have to sentimentalize over their own weaknesses or seek to justify them, which in the end is boring and one-sided. Overcoming their complexes, they hit accurately on what is most essential for human fate. I think the world should be so arranged that noble thinkers are physically fit and through this fitness superior to scoundrels. However, I'm afraid that meanwhile it's the other way around.

"Say what you like, but I'd like to have an Olympic medal. I would, and that's that," said Helena. "An Olympic medal or any other kind. Something of that sort. You can talk, but I don't believe you. It's very easy for a person to say that something isn't worth having if he happens to have it."

"Explain to me what use these medals would be to you."

"You don't understand a thing. I'd like to be someone other than the person I am. Can't you understand that?"

"Me not understand? What do you know about me, Helena? If I don't understand, then nobody in the world does."

"You too want to be someone different? No!"

"Someone else, or different. In any case, something of the sort torments me. Don't imagine you have a monopoly on that."

"Well, so who would you like to be?"

"It's hard for me to answer that definitely. Maybe a scientist carrying out unheard-of discoveries, a politician changing the maps of the world and the ruling customs, a builder of interplanetary vehicles. But basically that isn't important. I'm not concerned with a different profession, but rather with a different personality. Of course the two are connected. But it's the other personality that is really important. Funny thing. A person is devilishly attached to himself, but all he longs for is to be someone else. Isn't that funny? Tell me."

"I'm not attached to myself. I hate myself."

"You're only imagining it. That hatred is a side product of passionate love."

"You know, you're very bright. You really are. I never suspected it. When you talk I stop wondering whether what you say is right, I only listen."

"You exaggerate."

"I'd like to be bright. If it's my fate to be nothing other than what I am, then I'd like to be bright at least."

"You are."

"You only say so to put me off."

"The very fact that you ponder over all this is proof that you're bright."

"Oh go on with you. What of it? I don't know how to express any thought as wisely and strikingly as you do."

"Men know how to express themselves more concretely than women."

"I adore men. Men are impressive. Most of all they impress me precisely with their intelligence. Not at all by their looks. In general I eliminate good-looking men right away."

She started eyeing me. She gazed at me a long time, in such a way that I began feeling slightly ill at ease. I didn't know where to look, maybe I reddened a little. I thought it was time to take myself off.

"Tell me, Marek," said Helena, without shifting her gaze from me, "why is everything the way it is?"

I didn't quite know what this question referred to, but I replied as though I knew:

"Well, because that's the way it is, and there's no help for it."

"You know what I'd like. I'd like not to be Ksiezak's wife. Well, not to be. Don't make such a face. It isn't that I'd like to separate from Edward. I love him and basically my life with him is good. Despite his various faults, which you don't even know about, and despite the way his damn mother sticks her nose into everything. You can't even begin to picture to yourself how she poisons my life. What I said, about not wanting to be Mrs. Ksiezak, isn't directed against Edward at all. Rather against myself. You see? I disown myself. The self which I've become and consolidated. You see? To be someone entirely different. Even for a moment. Even from time to time."

I nodded, though I was only listening to what she was saying with half an ear. I wanted to go. I didn't know how to interrupt and tell her so. This unexpected intimacy with Helena embarrassed me. It wasn't at all unpleasant. But I was afraid that if I didn't leave at once, then the sudden connection between us would grow complex and break off. In order not to look at Helena, I started staring at the walls. I rested my gaze on a reproduction showing Leda and the swan. In my opinion it's junk, and highly tasteless into the bargain. It doesn't concern it that this picture is known and held in esteem. I don't remember too well who painted it. Rembrandt, Rubens? Tintoretto, maybe. God knows. I wanted to ask Helena, but it didn't seem right after she'd declared I was so unusually intelligent. It wasn't a question of the fear, through self-esteem, of putting my foot in it. But I didn't want to disappoint her. There's a *Leda and the Swan* by Leonardo da Vinci. But this wasn't it. Leonardo's *Leda* is a very beautiful picture. It was hanging in my room and Agnieszka didn't order me to take it down, though she gazed at it a while as though with some hesitation. She was probably wondering whether Leonardo da Vinci was sufficiently modern. Despite all, his authority won. Agnieszka had a thing about modernity. Leonardo's *Leda* was associated in my mind with massive architecture in an open space, whereas the *Leda* hanging in reproduction in the Ksiesaks' room made me think of a stuffy and clammy boudoir. It seems to me that sometimes love also is reminiscent of massive architecture in an open space, and then everything's all right. Nothing can become ambiguous or repulsive or clammy. Whatever happens takes on traits of massiveness. It's as simple and natural as nature. Such love happens rarely. People thirsty for pure and elevated love don't know enough, alas, to seek it where it must be sought; they're tempted by a stuffy, ambiguous boudoir. This ends with them becoming disgusted with what they'd regarded as the purest and most elevated. Then they start playing filthy tricks out of sheer fury.

Helena was talking, and I started to picture her in Leda's place. She was playing with the swan, not naked but in tight red pants and a black golf sweater. I watched as she expatiated with a serious expression on her face; since she was talking about basic matters, she tried to adopt a special dignity. This confused her, because she didn't realize what was going on behind her back. Meaning in my imagination, of course. But Helena's comicality started to make me somewhat uneasy. I realized that this wasn't ordinary schoolgirl comicality, as when one sticks a monkey cut out of paper to a schoolmate's jacket. It contained an element of playfulness, or maybe slyness, the giggle of a schoolgirl who, for the first time in her life, has gone to a movie which young people aren't allowed to see. This had an unhealthy effect on me. I had the urge to push her off her chair. To see her fall over onto the floor and roll there. Then to begin apologizing to her in an elegant and perfidious manner.

"It's really extraordinary," Helena was saying, "how wonderfully we understand one another. If it ever happens that I talk about such matters with Edward, he'll say, 'It's all because you don't do anything. If you worked, you wouldn't find the time to think about such nonsense.' Isn't that a dirty trick? Just tell me, isn't it dirty? In the first place, if I don't do anything, it's exclusively because of him. In the second, I slave at home from morning to night. Only for him. It's beastly treachery on his part to talk that way, isn't it? Oh, if you knew how all this sickens me. Why, really, can't a person change into someone else? Tell me! Why?"

"He can," I said, firmly.

"He can?" Helena was surprised.

"Absolutely."

"But how? Tell me!"

I didn't reply instantly, because I didn't quite know what to say.

"It needs some courage and determination," I said, in any case.

"What do you mean?"

She was staring at me inquiringly and uneasily. I turned my head away:

"Maybe I didn't express myself clearly. You need a little imagination."

"I have imagination, but what of that? My imagination is imprisoned in this apartment."

"You lack courage and determination."

"Oh, for goodness sake."

"Do you think you don't?"

"Certainly I lack them."

"Apart from that, one must have the art of yielding to moods. This is what the magic of the movies depends on. Sitting in a movie theater, everyone imagines he's the hero of the film. Providing the given hero corresponds, of course. This illusion can stretch beyond the time of the performance, in favorable circumstances. We see children who fight with one another as crusaders, cowboys, musketeers, who fall off roofs and break a leg like Zorro. But it's harder to discern the contests that various Gregory Pecks have with various Glen Fords, and various Marilyn Monroes with various Brigitte Bardots. The cinema screen is a strange frame, through which we watch a peculiar world. On the surface it's like ours, but as though contrary to it and awry. But a person must bring himself to go through this frame. As Alice went through the looking-glass in her room. Afterwards it's possible to roam about the land of enchantment. Anyone who can't get through that frame isn't a movie-goer but a slob. Too bad about the money he wasted on the ticket. Artur Wdowinski declares that the primary and perhaps the only function of the movies is to create in people the illusion that they're someone other than the person they are. Everything else in a movie is babble and humbug. And any subtle attempts to create an artistic movie for intellectual connoisseurs can only end in disaster. We are, it seems, witnesses of the start of this disaster right now."

I wasn't sure of the meaning of what I was saying. But it was of no consequence to me. I was trying to drive away with this jabbering the specter of Leda in tight pants and black golf sweater. Helena had leaned her cheek on her hand and was gazing at me, motionless. In her gaze I caught sight of something that aroused in me not only uneasiness but definite panic. I stood up instantly. She rose too. Not for a moment did she lower her gaze.

"Well, Helena," I said, trying to keep calm, "excuse me for staying so long and boring you with my chatter. Time to go."

"You speak very beautifully," said Helena, "it seems to me that in my life I've lost any amount of time doing various things instead of listening to you uninterruptedly. But don't think that I've discovered you only now."

She walked round the table and stopped in front of me.

"Remember how I pulled your hair at the dance?"

She pulled my hair and smiled.

Just the same as at the dance that time.

"Like that," she said. "Do you know why I did it?"

I knew now. But I didn't say anything. We gazed at each other. I could hear her breathing and could hear my own breathing. It became weirdly quiet in the room. I hadn't really believed it before, but people say that before death one sees one's entire life as if on a strip of film. At that moment I saw something exactly like that, with the difference that it didn't run backward, but forward. I could see, as on film, very accurately and with details, what was going to happen in a moment. Up to the very moment when I regretted what had happened, and once more in my life I would curse myself and spit in my own face. But that film was moving so rapidly that despite my knowing its inevitable ending I couldn't see any way to stop the desperate projection. Like swimmers at the starting post, we shivered and swayed toward each other. At this moment the phone rang. We stood for another moment, motionless. Then I silently indicated the ringing object. Helena bent her head and passed the back of one hand across her brow. The phone rang three times. The bell sounded quarrelsome and arrogant. I turned away and walked to the window. Nothing particular was happening outside. The shabby wall of the apartment house opposite, a cigarette kiosk, closed, and a fellow in the middle of the street, reading the "Sports Review." In the latest number an article had appeared, entitled: "Will Marek Arens, chameleon of the track, win over longer distances?" Helena kept repeating in an irritated voice: "Hello?" She even cursed in a way I would never have suspected of her. Why "chameleon of the track"? These journalists always think up God knows what, for effect.

Helena shouted into the phone:

"What is it, damn it . . . Will you finally get around to connecting us? This long-distance service is enough to drive anyone crazy . . . Well, at last! Is that you? Yes . . . yes, I say, it's me . . . It's me! Stop that senseless helloing . . . Yes, of course . . . Tomorrow morning? All right . . . all right . . . I paid it . . . yes . . . I did everything you told me to. Don't worry about a thing . . . Oh really, is it worth calling all the way from Warsaw

for such nonsense? Paid for by the Athletics Union? Oh. Marek?
No, because . . . He's here . . . Yes . . . He just arrived when
you called. Well, I called him, but he wasn't home all day . . .
Please don't yell your head off . . . if that isn't yelling, I don't
know what is . . ."

In a shameless manner, without any agreement with me, she
drew me into her lie, as if she considered we were conspirators in
a crime and must defend and attack together.

"For heaven's sake shut up! Please don't bother me with such
matters in the future . . . Maybe it's nothing big, but I'd prefer
you not to mix me up in your athletics nonsense . . . Soon you'll
be staying home to read the paper and make me train Marek.
Why do I have to be responsible for absolutely everything? Of
course he's listening. No, no! Take it easy. He isn't offended. In
any case, not with me . . . And why he should be with you, that I
really can't know . . . Tell me this, what's the use of calling from
Warsaw just to make a stupid scene? Go boil your head . . . Yes.
Twice, preferably . . . I'm not in the least upset, only I hate it
when you pick on me for no reason. Just like your mother . . .
Well, all right, darling, I'm not mad at you . . . Of course I'll get
breakfast ready for you, my tomcat . . . In a bowl. Well, in a
bowl for sure. What else do tomcats eat out of? Bye-bye, there's a
kiss for you . . . All right, I'll ask him right away . . ."

The man reading the "Sports Review" moved off slowly and
bumped into a girl who was rushing by. He put aside the paper,
turned around, and stared after her.

"Marek," said Helena, "Edward would like to talk to you. He's
calling from Warsaw."

She put the receiver down beside the phone and left the room.

"Hello," I said, and immediately said it again, because I said it
the first time in a sort of hoarse and strange voice.

"Hi, Marek. Excuse me. Helena has so much to do."

"But it wasn't her fault. I wasn't home since this morning."

"Really?"

"I'm telling you."

"Anyway, you've wasted your time on my account."

"But why are you making such a big thing out of it? Nothing
has happened."

"Whether or not . . . I like everything to go like clockwork.
But since you're not angry, it's all right. Did you find anything interesting in that book?"

"I don't think so. As far as running is concerned, there's not really anything new. Maybe in the vaulting. But I'm not an expert in that."

"Why is your voice so odd?"

"My voice odd? What do you mean?"

"Didn't catch cold, did you? Don't you start getting sick. I've got some good news for you. It's agreed that you start in the Memorial race for the three thousand."

"Really?"

"What, aren't you pleased?"

"I'm very pleased."

It didn't interest me in the slightest.

"You speak sort of indifferently."

"No, no, you're imagining it. Only you know . . . I'm a bit scared. I don't want to make a fool of myself."

"If you start approaching it like that, then I can promise you in advance that you'll make a fool of yourself. Man, what are you worried about? According to the times you make in training, you've got a chance not only of placing well, but of winning."

"Oh, winning, no less! I'll pray that I can run as far as the tape."

"What's wrong with you?"

"Nothing. I'm joking. Of course I'll win. I'll arrange a small colloquium for a select European stake."

"When you talk like that, then everything is OK. Now I know I can sleep easily. Well, goodbye, Marek, take care of yourself."

"Goodbye, old man. If you need anything, remember."

I put down the receiver and wondered what would happen when Helena came back into the room. She came in a moment later. Her hair combed somewhat differently, without the blue ribbon and with more make-up. She was holding a dustcloth in one hand, whistling and radiating with domestic energy. She cleared the tea glasses, wiped dust off the commode, straightened the chairs and began to meditate over a stain on the tablecloth.

"I'll be going," I said.

"What's your hurry?" she asked, and instantly began whistling again.

"I really am in something of a hurry. Our cooperative got an order for a set of store kiosks for Nowa Huta. They pushed it all on me. I've got a load of work."

No set of store kiosks existed and never would. Nobody dreamed of anything of the sort. Stagnation reigned in our building cooperative.

"I apologize to you again that you wasted your time on my account. Still more if you're so busy."

"It was really nothing. You don't have to talk about it so much. In any case, I intended to take a walk."

I wanted to add a stupid compliment to the effect that "If I've seen you, then my time has certainly not been wasted," but I immediately realized that in this particular situation it would be tactless, so I didn't say any more.

I went out, and she didn't stop me. She said goodbye to me politely but restrainedly. Just the way she greeted or said goodbye to me usually. One might have thought that I'd only gone to the Ksiezaks', found out that Ksiezak had gone away and left immediately, and nothing more had happened.

I went back home and didn't really know what to do. I sat down at the easel and began drawing. It bored me to tears. Fortunately my pencil broke. I regarded this as a reason for interrupting work.

I lay down on the couch and stared at the ceiling. Such a thing rarely happened to me. By nature I was vigorous, active, and hated immobility. But this time, uneasiness prevented me from taking up anything definite. I thought lying down would let me unwind. But I didn't feel any relaxation. Something had started to happen. The ordinary and conventional goodbye with Helena was a fact devoid of meaning. The projection of the film of events not yet shot was proceeding, somehow or other. The gong had saved me from a knockout, but the fight wasn't ended. Here fate had foisted on me a very excellent opportunity to make a pig of myself again. This time for all times and finally. What would have happened if the phone hadn't rung? It's not possible to state with absolute certainty that I wouldn't have come to my senses. A man rescued from an airplane crash is alive. And that's what counts, not that he might possibly, under different and less fortunate circumstances, be dead. Fate had foisted on me an opportunity to make a pig of myself. Why shouldn't it have been rather an opportunity for mastering the swine in me? The struggle was starting. Yes. The struggle was assuredly starting. As usual before a fight, I felt peculiar excitement. A hotness which begins in the neighborhood of the stomach and flows through the whole body. I experienced this feeling strongest before the start of the Olympics finals, when I dislocated my foot immediately after the start. Then, alone in the dressing room, I cried for a long time; this is something nobody knew or ever found out. I don't know why. All that wasn't really so very important to me. But whether it matters or not, a fight is a fight, and such a feeling of terrible excitement before the start is a good feeling. And I won't forget too that Dorota rushed to me that time and she was entirely different from the way she usually was. She put her arms around my head and pressed me strongly to her breasts. She, who is totally disinclined to giving way to feelings, who knows nothing about tenderness and has never heard of it. But that gesture of hers had nothing to do with feelings or tenderness. She knows what a fight is and understands fighting. It was only a sporting gesture. Just as the Soviet runner Krepyatkin once pressed my head to his chest immediately after a race in which we carried on a murderous struggle and he won at the tape by a few inches. But that time I had a good chance for the Olympics and everyone knew it, and maybe such a chance would never occur again. I had an irrepressible longing to go back to Helena. To see her even if only for a moment. To phone her and hear her voice. I wasn't able to define what had passed between us. Particularly as nothing had passed between us, really. Strictly speaking, nothing had happened. Provided of course that I didn't take into account the fact that at the very thought of Helena I grew hot and cold by turns. Where had all this suddenly come from? Why Helena all of a sudden? Helena who used to seem totally uninteresting to me, and whom I didn't like much. How in the world can nature play such insane jokes? The fight was beginning. A hellish fight, not to be evaded by dislocating one's foot. The desire to go back to Helena, to see her just for a moment, was growing within me. And I realized that the more it grew and the more it would grow, the more strongly I would resolve not to see her and not allow anything to happen between us. But isn't that stupid, really? Why am I erecting this building which won't serve anyone for shelter? People have agreed among themselves long ago that certain matters would be settled stealthily and on the sly, and as long as it's done stealthily and on the sly, one must admit that nothing bad happens to anyone. To go back to Helena, grapple with her in an embrace, in accordance with the demands of fate, which at the call of nature had taken on a fighting attitude. I knew that afterwards everything would end, that the entirely accidentally lost Leda in red pants and black golfing sweater would melt away in space. A feeling of defilement and degradation would remain, but it wouldn't last long. Humanity long ago found out excellent means for doing away quickly and efficiently with such feelings. If I didn't do that, if I defended myself, then it would only be in order to transform a trivial little comedy into a monumental drama and to make Leda in red pants and black golfing sweater, who was only a merry naiad, into an elevated and unique goddess of love. Calmly, calmly. None of the wisest and most logical arguments are of any use. I won't yield! I'll fight not to be a swine. I'll fight, so as not to betray a friend and keep true to the girl to whom I promised that. What for? I don't know. Just as I don't know why I fight desperately to the end when on the race track, at a time when it's not a question of any stake and winning doesn't matter. I told Agnieszka she's the last girl with whom I'd link myself in life. That I'd remain true to her whatever happened. I told her this not only because at that time I loved her, but primarily because I was already too weary of general unfaithfulness, my own and other people's. Of the general chicanery and tyranny of illusions which command us to adore on bended knee that which afterwards becomes an object of boredom, sometimes even of hate and antipathy.

Two days had passed since the night when Agnieszka came to my place from the club dance, but she gave no sign of life. I couldn't understand it. After all, it was merely good manners to take some sort of interest in me. Girls consider that men have obligations toward them, even if they only stroll with them in the park. They themselves feel under no obligations. In any case, I considered this problem from the point of view of social customs and formalities, for the sole purpose of increasing my regret and soothing my longing for Agnieszka. Then again, I was certain that this was precisely the sort of love which every person tries to find, that Agnieszka was the being destined to me by fate and God, if anything like fate and God exists, which I personally doubt. I walked around Cracow feeling blue, lost in thought, incapable of work or effort. The weather was awful. It was cloudy, and dirty, clammy snow obstructed the roads and sidewalks. Properly speaking there wasn't any day at all. An unbroken night persisted, broken briefly by a gloomy dusk. I could of course have found Agnieszka through Dr. Plucinski, or have found out about her at the Academy or through the President. But I didn't intend to do this. If she didn't want me, why should I look for her? I never learned how to conquer women. It seemed to me ill-judged and humiliating. Most women want to be conquered and in this connection indulge in various tomfooleries, often leading men to irritation and estrangement. Only professional collectors, habitual card-sharpers of love of this kind, individuals who make it a point of honor to lead unfortunate coquettes from displays of indifference to hidden intrusiveness. But normal men have neither the time nor the head for such things. As for me I could go out to meet a woman only in the event of her being ready to meet me halfway. I didn't have time to play around with any nonsense. I've noticed that professional seducers, lovers of conquering fortresses supposedly unconquerable, sooner or later get into unpleasant trouble. Whether as exploiters or as damaged. All of this of course hadn't and couldn't have any connection with Agnieszka. But precisely because it had no connection with her, I had to make up my mind to avoid being aggressive toward her and not to look for her if she didn't wish to see me. I had to consider that she had come to my place under the influence of the mood and the liquor she'd drunk. When she later realized this, shame and distaste overcame her. If she still wanted anything in connection with me, it was only not to meet me again. It was hard to explain her behavior in any other way. But, explaining it in this way, it was hard for me to look for her or to seek an accidental meeting with her. I was suffering because all together this wasn't such a simple matter. If it had only been a question of Agnieszka! But what was there to do? I'd accidentally met a girl to whom I hadn't at first paid much attention, who later seemed sweet, and finally so very sweet that I'd have liked to stay with her longer, if not forever. But it turned out that this girl didn't want me at all. No help for that. I'd suffer for some time, suffering conventionally as all disappointed lovers do. Then the suffering would end too. But Jowita was involved in all this. Jowita, whom I hadn't stopped thinking about for a moment, from the time I met her. Although I was trying to cheat myself, Jowita, who was sufficiently unreal for me so that I could love other women while thinking of her, and sufficiently verifiable in my memories for me to imagine her as a living, existing ideal. The fact is that I never stopped thinking about Jowita. I thought about her through everything that happened around me. As a pious monk thinks of God and eternal life during his everyday tasks, not excepting occupations as exceptional and desultory as hidden dissipation. I thought of her while loving Agnieszka and loving Helena, I thought about her while in the bath before the concert, fearing I'd be late; it was damnably late and an unspeakable quarrel was in the offing, but I didn't want to get out of the water.

I cudgeled my brains. The next night, when Agnieszka came to me, I didn't sleep or hardly slept at all. Pondering over all this I came to the positive and irrefutable conclusion: Agnieszka was Jowita. I thought about Agnieszka when I came back from the walk during which I carried out that one-sided conversation with her. I lay down and then began fancying various things such as one fancies before falling asleep. Among them loomed Jowita. She came up to my bed, leaned over me and took the veil from her face. I saw the face of Agnieszka. But after all, that wasn't why I came to the conclusion that Agnieszka was Jowita. I realized I was starting time and again to do things that placed my reason under a serious question mark. However, I wasn't yet so stupid as to form an opinion about phenomena according to visions seen in a half-sleep. The visions merely drove me to wonder which was Agnieszka, and which Jowita. No matter how I tried to think of this, no matter how I tried to compare and relate the facts, it worked out for me as though in an account which has been minutely checked several times: Agnieszka *is* Jowita. Everything pointed to it. Everything except the perhaps unclear matter with Mika, which however would assuredly be explained in a simple way. Should it ever come to an explanation. For Agnieszka had vanished. And she'd vanished just as Jowita had vanished after the dance. The entire matter was a prank for Agnieszka-Jowita, but it had gone too far and she considered it proper to break it off. So I was suffering, and it wasn't the common, conventional suffering. I was suffering on account of two girls, not one. For although I was convinced that Agnieszka and Jowita were one and the same person, yet somehow I separated them in my thoughts. Really, it was difficult to explain this matter properly. I myself didn't understand it well, although to me it was obvious. I think that it will be simplest to compare it to the mystery of the Holy Trinity.

So two days had passed since that stupid dance at the club and the beautiful night spent with Agnieszka. On the morning of the third day I decided to shake myself out of it. Sometimes a person takes such firm decisions. He feels an upsurge of energy, anger against everything that is preventing him from living, the will to remove it all from his way. Such a state of inner effort usually lasts only a short time. It is reminiscent of the visions called up by the effect of alcohol. A person suddenly decides to become a Boy Scout or a coal miner, to flee into the wilderness and live the life of primitive people, or to stop thinking of himself and devote himself exclusively to his family. It seems completely natural that he wants this, completely obvious that he'll carry it out; but when the alcohol stops working and his head starts to ache, he thinks of nothing else but how to get rid of his hangover. As for me, I never made any decisions under the influence of alcohol. However, when I made them in a sober condition, nothing could induce me to withdraw. I had the will and resistance which more than once led me into overdoing things. It happened, for instance, that I started solving a crossword puzzle out of boredom. Then, although I no longer felt like it, I worked on it to the end, irritable with myself and wasting any amount of time in vain. So, when I decided to shake myself loose from all these entanglements concerned with Agnieszka, I meant it. It wasn't to tempt and provoke fate in the completely opposite direction. Even perfectly serious people often do that. In the morning I went to our cooperative. There I displayed so much vigor and energy that I reduced the workshop to a state of complete confusion. Sudden and unexpected things, even if they represent the most positive elements, usually act destructively. People get accustomed to the status quo, and changes for the better reduce them to just the same confusion as changes for the worse. I'm trying to avoid generalizing. So in this case too I don't claim it's always the same everywhere. But it's often so. And it certainly was so then in our workshop. Anyway, maybe this doesn't bear particularly favorable witness to the regard which my creative invention enjoys there. In any case, for some ten days, that is to say from the meeting with Jowita at the Academy of Fine Arts ball, I did nothing, or practically nothing. Now, with unheard-of enthusiasm I revealed the wish to make up for lost time. I criticized everything that had been done during my absence. I put forward new ideas of my own. I subjected the organization of work in our cooperative to general criticism. My colleagues stared at me and for a while said nothing. First to speak was Michal Podgorski:

"You know what, Marek," he said, "if you've already had your say sufficiently, then take a pencil, sit down at your easel and buckle down to that piece of work which we've been waiting for with impatience and longing for several days."

Shame overcame me. I went on, merely for the sake of saying something:

"As you wish. But by the time you convince yourselves that my remarks were justified, it'll be too late. I ask only one thing: don't come to me repenting and saying that you should have listened to me."

"We promise," cried Michal. "We promise, and you can rest assured that we'll keep the promise."

Everyone laughed, and so did I. What was I to do? I set to work immediately. Of course, I'd made a fool of myself. In our cooperative, I was in charge of tackling technical assignments. I did this well. But I didn't have much to say in more basic matters. And I had no ambitions in that direction. That was Michal Podgorski's sphere. He was making his mark. He was talked of more and more in Poland. He was talented and won many competitions. In each competition he took me on as collaborator. I knew how to be grateful. Michal had been a typical bungler. We made friends in the department during studies. I helped him a great deal. I really ought to say that he was a bungler then. Later, probably not. He stopped being one thanks to me. It wasn't a question of my forcing him to train. He hurled the javelin quite well. More important was the fact that I taught him to look on the world with a man's eyes, and to behave like a man. If it hadn't been for me he'd probably have gone to the dogs. He didn't have an easy life. His father had been an officer between the wars and, what was worse, was making a fool of himself by emigrating. At the time we were studying, the custom still prevailed that people answered for the sins of their fathers. Michal kept having misunderstandings with the League of Polish Youth, although nothing linked him with his father. Except that he despised him. He had a right to. His father had stopped concerning himself with him and his mother, whom he'd left behind when he ran away abroad. In a word, they wanted to throw Michal out of the department on account of his father, who was an utter swine toward Michal. I stood up in his defense at a meeting. I, who represented my country with a white eagle on my chest and didn't represent it badly. It sounded stupid and I was ashamed to speak that way. But I had to. It brought results. It so happened that a few days earlier there had been a contest with the Hungarians, at which I'd effectively mowed down our "nephews." So they let Michal alone. I liked the way he didn't say anything to me after that meeting. He just came up to me and gave me his hand. Just as one shakes the hand of a partner after a fight. He didn't apologize or get sentimental. I also helped him a little financially. At that time my father and I were competing in selling off various family valuables and souvenirs. He for vodka, I for my studies. I also got "cadre money" from the Polish Athletic Association. Michal kept a record of it all and paid it back to the last penny when he started earning. He was a genuine friend. Properly speaking, I had few friends. Who, for example? Ksiezak, Szymaniak as long as he was still alive, Dorota, Artur Wdowinski to a certain extent. I'd call him a sidekick rather than a friend. Out of them all, however, the most genuine friend was Michal. Even though we saw each other rarely outside the workshop. He was busy all the time and didn't have time for nonsense, but I did. That must be admitted. He impressed me: he had everything I lacked. He was intelligent, with the sort of intelligence of a reader of wise books. My intelligence was at most that of a naïve reasoner. I realized this. Sometimes I spoke perfectly to the point, until I wondered where I had got it from. But then again sometimes I talked nonsense. As for example that time in the workshop. Michal was an expert on art. He was skilled in various subtleties of life which I could barely sense. Michal was a person of high caliber. One of those people who in principle get on my nerves and by whom Agnieszka was delighted. But despite this he just didn't get on my nerves. I admired him. In many matters he was the highest authority for me. Besides, he was the only one of my friends whom Agnieszka respected. He too behaved toward her with particular attention. When they were together they got on my nerves somewhat, however. The conversations they carried on sounded a little artificial. I had the impression that Michal was attempting, out of politeness more than anything else, to adjust to the high level which Agnieszka required. I wondered how it was possible that at the ball, then at my place and for a little while longer, she managed to be such a fine, simple girl. But suddenly she changed into a pretentious reader of the literary journals, a virtual disputant of contrived matters of no use to anyone.

That day in the workshop I tackled several days' worth of work. Michal was pleased and said, "I couldn't cope with this without you." I pretended to accept this as something perfectly natural. Besides, when I really got down to work, few could keep pace with me. Michal and I were really well integrated. It is true that it wouldn't have been easy for him without me. In the afternoon I went out for training; I hadn't been in the club for quite a few days either. I exercised as eagerly as I'd worked in the morning. And I thought to myself that the best thing to do is to take a turn of work properly, and to train regularly. It wasn't worth bothering one's head with other things. On the way back from training, I met Agnieszka.

I swear I'd have retreated if I'd had the time. I didn't want to meet her accidentally. I wanted her to come to me. To telephone, at least. I admit I wanted nothing as much as that. I was able to stifle my longing with work and training. But I couldn't get rid of it entirely. At least, not in one day. I wanted to see her. This was all I wanted. But not by the kindness of fate. So I swear I'd have retreated and made off, had I been able to. However, we met the moment I was turning the corner from July Manifesto Street into Straszewski Street. We almost collided.

"Oh, good afternoon," she said. It didn't look as though she was startled, impressed or even taken aback by the meeting. She said "Good afternoon" quite simply, as one says it to an accidentally met acquaintance who is unconnected by more intimate relations. I almost fainted. The phrase "I almost fainted" belongs to the exclamations often used in a symbolic manner. But I really almost fainted. It's an understandable thing that the more violently I tried that day to remove Agnieszka from my consciousness, the greater was the shock of this meeting. Fortunately I had lots of experience in taking blows. Sometimes I received a real bomb, after which I knew only one thing and held instinctively to one thought: not to let it be seen that I had felt the blow. And this is why I succeeded, despite everything, in not fainting at the sight of Agnieszka. I controlled myself and said as indifferently as she:

"Good afternoon."

She was holding a cylinder in one hand. She began shifting it.

"I'm very happy to see you," she said. "Which way are you going? Maybe you'll accompany me a little way?"

"I'd gladly accompany you, but I'm in a bit of a hurry."

"Too bad. I'm in a hurry too. Otherwise I'd have accompanied you."

She was in the same short black fur jacket but on her head she wore a beret. A navy-blue Basque beret. I thought to myself that if now for no reason whatsoever I were to jerk it off her head, that would be something. I'd cause her surprise, maybe fright. Maybe she'd start to run away, crying, like Alina that time. In any case, I'd force her to express some sort of attitude toward me. She was fearfully indifferent. Indifferent and, what was worse, polite. This awakened helpless rage in me. I had had dealings with many girls, but no girl had ever behaved to me in this way. Who knows whether I wouldn't really have jerked that beret off her head. Suddenly however I recalled that Agnieszka is the niece of Dr. Plucinski, the president of our club. This stopped me. Not until later did I realize that this fact was laughable proof of my enslavement by sports. Generally speaking, none of us like the officials in or outside the club very much. We have a sort of undefined feeling that we have to work against them. But we also have the feeling that we're in their hands. They determine our fates. They can always find a pretext for not entering us in an important match, for disqualifying us, for not sending us abroad, for causing various unpleasantnesses. In general the opinion prevails that it's best not to say too much and not to get unnecessarily involved. Artur claims it's just the same in the theater. There were those who felt they were too strong, and that ended badly for them. A year or even a six-month disqualification for unbecoming conduct and lack of discipline. Who could prove that such a disqualification was undeserved and unjust? I don't give a damn for officials, and sports is of no consequence to me. As it is, I'm going to drop it all soon. But I instinctively feel generally disciplined by the club and terrorized from above. At a meeting in Stuttgart, I saw the movie *Spartacus,* about gladiators. I thought to myself that those strong men allowed themselves to be directed by a few bunglers just as we do. When they tried to rebel, it ended unhappily for them. All the same, I quite like Dr. Plucinski. He's not the worst of the officials. But pulling off his niece's beret would have to qualify as an infringement of sports discipline. A foul, the act of a hooligan on the sports ground. The matter would have to be considered by the appropriate club or even union committee. If I were to tell anyone all this in this manner, I'd most probably be considered an idiot. However, it's necessary to take into consideration, first, that I'm exaggerating a little, and second, that the thoughts on this matter coursed through my head during the space of a few seconds while I was in a state of acute upset. Which, furthermore, I was trying to conceal. Apart from this, things told look entirely different from things experienced. People, generally speaking, fantasize incredibly. Which doesn't in the least mean they're raving. They themselves can't really tell what happened in reality and what they invented later when they consider some event, comparing its actual course with a course it might have taken, or which in their opinion it ought to have taken. It's possible that I thought about that beret and the matters connected with sports discipline later. But in the end what significance does that have? The essential thing is that I was reduced to despair and grim determination by Agnieszka's indifference. I felt the terrible need of some sort of physical violence which would force her to adopt an emotional attitude. But most of all what mattered to me was that she was to guess nothing. This is why I was trying to adopt the attitude rather of a habitual seducer, for whom a meeting with importunate girls was daily routine. If it can be called that.

"Well, goodbye," I said. "It was very nice meeting you."

Agnieszka stood a while in silence. She was gazing at the tips of her shoes and playing with the cylinder, which almost dropped from her hands. I desperately wanted it to fall. To fall into the mud on the sidewalk and get really soiled. It was assuredly some work from the Academy which she was having to do again. She grabbed it nimbly at the last moment. She looked into my eyes and said:

"Goodbye."

It seemed to me that she wanted to say something more. Her mouth was half open and her eyes narrowed. However, she said nothing. She turned and walked away. I was really in despair. More despairing than I'd ever supposed that it was possible to be. That wasn't Agnieszka. The look of those narrowed eyes was the gaze of Jowita. If I ever again doubted that Agnieszka was Jowita, the doubt would have been finally dispelled at that moment. For an instant I saw only her eyes. The same eyes that had gazed at me at dawn in the Academy. When she had said, "You'll get what you want. I'll run and change. Wait by the gate."

And she had run down the hallway.

Why was this girl playing such uncanny pranks on me? Like a devil in a fairy tale on a condemned soul. Was she really playing pranks on me? It seems that the matter must be regarded as far simpler than I wanted to see it. Fate brought me into contact with Agnieszka by accident, without the participation of her will. Under the influence of the mood and of vodka she came to me that night. Now she couldn't forgive herself for that. She didn't want to see me any more. That was simple.

I stood a while longer at that accursed corner. As though waiting for Agnieszka, who had turned into July Manifesto Street, to come back and tell me I was mistaken. That she loved me, wanted to stay with me. But I wasn't waiting. I knew she was going into the dusk with that cylinder of hers. She was walking fast. Maybe she was hoping to meet someone whom she wanted to placate on account of what had happened with me. In any case, she wouldn't come back. She wouldn't return to me. She wanted to be as far away from me as possible. Not as close as possible.

The instinct, for that is surely what it must be called, the instinct to explain all phenomena to one's own advantage is surely one of the strongest instincts rooted in man. At least as strong as the maternal instinct. Whatever facts might say or common sense dictate, man always yields in the end for longer or shorter periods to the treacherous promptings of this instinct. Generally he makes a madman of himself by this; less often it turns out that the instinct was healthy and should really have been yielded to.

When I woke up next morning, I started thinking about Agnieszka. That was my first thought every morning. But this time I came to the conclusion that I'd been behaving like a hysterical old woman. After pondering over it all soberly, coolly, and dispassionately, it was necessary to reach obvious conclusions. I considered that Agnieszka was avoiding me and didn't want any more relations with me. What sort of proof did I have that she didn't consider the same in relation to me? Misunderstandings of this kind between people in love are typical and classical. Often something of the sort is seen in the movies and at the theater. Almost every love intrigue in Molière is based on this. All the same, I must admit that all that seemed devilishly stupid and naïve to me. And Molière neither diverted nor amused me. Mainly I pitied him quite privately. Apparently all his life he had terrible trouble with his wife, who was a complete floozy and harlot.

Why did he stick to her so stubbornly? It was instinct. This accursed instinct to explain everything to one's own advantage induced him to do so. I wager it. I'd sooner not go down in history at all rather than with the stigma of being a whining cuckold, even in addition to being a genius.

But didn't Agnieszka have the right to consider I'd treated her lightly? To think to herself that I'd had enough of her after that one night? That I wanted to get rid of her? And didn't she have the right to expect, when she left, that I'd want to accompany her? That I'd ask when we'd see each other? Ask for her phone number? I felt it was necessary to separate without a word, without any questions. It seemed to me that the mood of the moment required this, and that Agnieszka assuredly wanted that. But it wasn't put into words at all that I sensed this was how it must be. Even if it had been? I ought to have looked for her afterwards and not passively expected her to look for me. It was entirely clear and obvious that I'd behaved like a moron. Never did anyone rejoice in his life, surely, to discover he'd behaved like a moron, as I did then. Agnieszka was certainly suffering. She was suffering because of me, just as I was suffering because of her. And what was it all for? Why prolong the stupid, Molière-like scene of amorous mistakes? I decided to find Agnieszka.

I went to the club house in the hope of finding Dr. Plucinski. He was there. But he was playing bridge. It was difficult for me to go up to him out of the blue, and ask about Agnieszka in front of the others. These officials are continually playing bridge. I don't know when they find the time to concern themselves with sports, not to mention professional matters. Personally, if I were sick, I'd rather not go to Dr. Plucinski to be cured. I was lucky, for just then he spread out his cards and got up from the table for a minute.

"Good to see you, Doctor," I went up to him, "I have a very small request."

This opening, with this "very small request," wasn't very adroit. But it was all the same to me. As it was, I was ready for his stupid jokes.

"I'm listening, Marek," he said, "I'm always glad to do anything for you. Do you need money? I can help you with a small loan."

"Not at all. . . . Could you give me Agnieszka's phone number? I promised to find a book for her . . . that book about . . . about Leonardo da Vinci. I've just found it, but I lost her phone number. Could you . . ."

"Of course," said Dr. Plucinski. He took out a notebook and began looking. He didn't evince the slightest disposition for stupid jokes, although by my embarrassment and stuttering I'd given him direct cause. I was grateful to him for this. "Five, seventy-seven, thirteen. But no. Agnieszka isn't in Cracow."

"How come?"

"Quite simple. She left. Five, seventy-seven, thirteen. Yes. I don't know. She doesn't report to me particularly. She went to Warsaw to arrange matters connected with her journey to the States. She'll be back tomorrow or next day. Marek, are you seriously thinking of long distances?"

"I don't think anything. Ksiezak thinks for me."

"Do you consider that enough?"

"Entirely. I can run a hundred and twenty, I can run eight hundred, one thousand five hundred, five thousand, ten thousand, I can vault or hurl the discus, and if anybody absolutely wanted, I can also run eight hundred meters through women's gossip."

"Why are you hamming it up so, Marek?"

"I'm not hamming it up."

"We want you to run three thousand at the Memorial. What do you think of this?"

"I can run. Why not?"

"But what's your opinion of it?"

"I haven't any. I'll run and that's that."

"Oh dear, Marek, Marek. Somehow you're out of sorts today. Fortunately I know you. But that number: five, seventy-seven, thirteen."

"Five, seventy-seven, thirteen. Thank you, Doctor."

"Write it down or you'll forget it."

"I won't forget."

"Well then, goodbye."

"Goodbye, Doctor."

I went back home. On the way I repeated: five, seventy-seven, thirteen. I lifted the receiver and dialed this number. I knew Agnieszka wasn't there, but I wanted at least to hear the tone which would resound as ringing in her empty room. Maybe it was silly and romantic, but I'd been reduced to a romantic state. Hardly had I dialed the number when someone lifted the receiver. I hadn't expected this at all. I took fright and almost put my receiver down.

"Hello," I heard a woman's voice.

"Sorry," I said, "wrong number."

"How do you know it's a wrong number?"

"It's a wrong number. I know."

"But whom did you want to talk to?"

"Isn't it a matter of indifference, since it's a wrong number?"

"You must be a conceited person, peremptory and self-assured. A tyrant at home as well. I wouldn't like to be your wife."

"It seems to me that at this moment no such danger threatens you."

"Ah, you have greatly reassured me."

"I'm glad to have reassured you. Goodbye and excuse me."

"Don't mention it. But whom did you want to speak to?"

"Why does that interest you?"

"You know, you're an odd person. You call me up, and then it surprises you that I'm interested who it is you want to speak to."

"I'm not calling you at all."

"Strictly speaking, you are."

"How come you're so certain?"

"Facts speak for themselves."

"The best proof that appearances are deceptive. It's a wrong number."

"How stubborn you are."

"Not so much as to take up so much of your time unnecessarily. Thank you for the very pleasant chat and goodbye."

"Where did you get my phone number from, you silly?"

"What?"

"I'm asking you, you silly, where you got my phone number from? From uncle Plucinski?"

"Really, Agnieszka!"

"I said that the facts give the appearance you're calling me. Are you always so stubborn?"

"How did it happen that I didn't recognize your voice?"

"It surprises me, too."

"I couldn't suppose I'd find you at home. That's why."

"Obviously. That justifies you entirely. If one calls up a person, it's not possible to suppose that one will find that person at home."

"You were supposed to have gone to Warsaw."

"I was and I'm going. Of course, provided I'm not late on account of stupid phone calls. Could you explain to me why you're calling me up if you think I'm in Warsaw?"

"No, I can't."

"Sometimes one does things which one can't explain to oneself afterward. Not even to oneself. Isn't it so? Well, tell me. Why don't you speak?"

"Are you angry with me for calling you?"

"No. I'm very glad."

"Is that sincere?"

"Yes. I was sorry you didn't call."

"But after all you could have called me."

"Yes, I could have."

"And you didn't."

"No . . . Marek, I'm late."

"What time does your train leave?"

"In a half hour."

"Can I see you off?"

"If you want."

"I do."

"The Warsaw Express, platform six, first-class smoker. I must apologize to you."

"What for?"

"I deliberately altered my voice a little when I heard you on the phone. You're not mad?"

"No. But why did you do that?"

"How should I know? I just did."

"Sometimes one does things which one can't explain to oneself afterward. Not even to oneself. Isn't it so?"

"No. Just for a joke. I was glad you were calling. For goodness sake! Marek, I'm late. See you. Thanks for calling."

She slammed down the receiver.

I saw Agnieszka off on the train and it was beautiful. Not in the railroad station, obviously. In the railroad station there was fog, that hopeless Cracow fog, dirty and clammy, which makes you want to wash it off the sidewalks, streets, and walls. With soap and a stiff brush. But it was beautiful, because we walked along the platform arm in arm and Agnieszka behaved marvellously, like Catherine in Hemingway's *A Farewell to Arms*. Agnieszka also told me to read this book, and I must confess that this was one of the few books Agnieszka told me to read which I read through to the end. Not only did I read it to the end, but with great pleasure. Only out of contrariness did I tell Agnieszka it was boring. To which she shrugged. I adore Hemingway and have read everything he wrote. But I rather suspect he's a hidden bungler. He's too excited by descriptions of battles, boxing, and bullfights. Even though he describes these things splendidly too, I imagine him, I don't know why, as a boy playing with lead soldiers. But in the final analysis this isn't too important. He understands men's affairs.

Agnieszka and I walked along the platform, I bought her magazines for the journey, and oranges which quite by accident were to be found in the station kiosk. There was no mention by either of us of any misunderstandings. We behaved like a couple long attached and able to understand one another. I was sure Agnieszka was glad I was seeing her off, and she felt as good in this fog-soiled railroad station as I. She said: "Go before the train leaves. I can't bear the sorrow that comes over me when a train leaves and someone stands on the platform and waves."

"Someone?"

"You."

"Then, till we meet again, Agnieszka."

She reached up on tiptoe and kissed me. I wanted her to say something more. I wanted this terribly. She said:

"Behave yourself properly, don't flirt with girls, and wait nicely for me to come back."

"When are you coming back?"

"Day after tomorrow. I'll call you right away. Goodbye."

"Goodbye."

I wanted to say "goodbye, darling," but somehow it didn't fit. So I didn't add anything to that "goodbye," only walked away. I walked quickly toward the exit and didn't look back. I have the idea that the hero of *A Farewell to Arms,* whose first name and surname I just can't remember at this moment, walked away at the Milan railroad station exactly like this. He walked away exactly the same that time when he saw Catherine off on the train in Milan. Good God, what a boob I am! After all it was she who saw him off, not he her!

The moments of relaxation after dissensions with a loved girl have been followed by reconciliation are truly marvelous. Unfortunately, life is made up of relaxations but also of tensions. One follows the other inevitably. Relaxations can't exist of their own accord. On the other hand, I'm afraid that nothing but tensions can, and the lives of some unlucky persons consist of nothing but tensions. But I think this is largely their own fault. I've observed that unlucky guys are always terrible egoists. I never met an unlucky guy who was altruistic. They're so terribly absorbed in their own fate and so suspiciously prejudiced against what it brings and offers that it's precisely on this account that they cause that acute state of permanent tension. I don't think I ought to be included in their ranks. I've experienced tensions and relaxations quite often, with a considerable preponderance of relaxations. But as I walked out of the railroad station, I thought to myself that Agnieszka's train had already left. I was traveling with her in a first-class smoker, with her magazines and oranges. Each moment she was going further and further away from me. I felt that various doubts were overcoming me and that the marvelous feeling of calm and confidence which I had experienced on the platform was beginning to desert me. Agnieszka's behavior, despite its appearance of tenderness, awoke doubts in me after my parting from her. I felt that something was lacking in her attitude toward me. I didn't sense this tenderness directly but rather as though through some sort of thick and soft veil. If I had to compare Agnieszka yet again to Catherine in *A Farewell to Arms,* then I'd say she didn't so much recall her as act her part wonderfully. But this wasn't what aroused my greatest uneasiness. In the final analysis, one always lives through this kind of doubt when something starts with a girl, and it's precisely here that the system of tensions and relaxations works most energetically. Walking through the public gardens toward Hospital Street, I entertained this kind of doubt regarding Agnieszka, but by the time I reached Little Market Place I was suddenly able to find dazzling counterarguments which would put me back in a state of joyful inebriation. What started to make me uneasy was much more serious and had its basic link primarily with me, and only indirectly with Agnieszka. Anyway, I'm not too sure it's indirect. Can it be called that? Everything happening in my life now revolved around Agnieszka and concerned primarily her. For or against. And it was precisely Agnieszka, no one else, who had become the cause of what was surely the first resignation from a fight in all my life. No matter what happened, I always fought to a finish. Sometimes I experienced hard times in the ring; sometimes the track burned my feet. Even that time at the Olympics, I kept running with a dislocated foot until I lost consciousness and fell down. The doctors simply couldn't understand how it had happened that I could run three hundred meters after dislocating my foot, and our masseur Mietek Feigenblatt said, "Such a miracle could only happen in Rome." But now I surrendered. I surrendered for the first time in my life. After all, I'd decided to shake myself free of anything connected with Agnieszka, to forget her, and to return to normal life. And on top of that I boasted to myself of my obstinacy and willpower. Of the certitude that nothing was able to prevail on me to withdraw once I'd decided something. And then, not even knowing how or when, nor caring about the new and unexpected defeat I had experienced on the corner of Straszewski and July Manifesto Streets, I began looking for Agnieszka. I'd found her. And it seemed, apparently, that I was right in breaking through my obstinacy. But I couldn't consider this as entirely right. The feeling that I'd yielded, surrendered, lost harassed me. But when a man surrenders, nothing good can come of it for him. One must be consistent. Even at a time when it seems only unthinking obstinacy. The power of consistency reaches far and is not easy to pin down. This is how I thought about it all after seeing Agnieszka off at the station. What did it matter that in the end I started to think of nothing but that she'd return the day after tomorrow, on Wednesday? That I would see her. This thought at first stifled and then drove away all other thoughts.

But on Wednesday I waited in vain for a phone call. Again on Thursday. I thought that maybe business had detained her in Warsaw. Dr. Plucinski, whom I met at the club, mentioned in passing that he'd seen Agnieszka the previous day. It turned out, a great deal sooner than might have been expected, that he who surrenders must experience nothing but bitterness and humiliation. That consistency in action is something on which one always wins. Despite this, I couldn't give up hope and kept waiting for the call. At last, the phone rang early Friday morning. But it was my mother's bungler of a doctor, calling to say my mother had died suddenly that night of a heart attack.

This news had a strange effect on me. It didn't overwhelm me in the sense of feelings. I wasn't overwhelmed in the least. The only strong sensation I experienced at that moment was one of disappointment. That it was Mother's doctor who'd called, not Agnieszka. Of course I had to pretend to be terribly upset, even desperate and shattered. This irritated and tortured me, but what else could I do? I couldn't stand hypocrisy and was of the opinion that there are no circumstances that justify it. Except of course in cases when speaking the truth amounts to boorishness. Anyway, I've noticed that those enemies of hypocrisy who don't refrain even from boorishness in the name of truth and sincerity, turn out sooner or later to be the most skilled money-grabbers and will sell their own brother for the dubious value of worldly profits. Of course I couldn't say to my mother's doctor, "Oh, leave me alone, what does it matter to me at this time? I want Agnieszka to call, and I don't give a damn about anything else." That would have been the truth, but I couldn't say it. And not only because I didn't want to behave like a boor toward the doctor. But slowly I began to realize that it was also a question of something else, of something much more important, although perhaps a little unclear.

I think that if I were to admit how I took the news of my mother's death, most people would treat me with indignation and deep distaste. Few would agree to accept as justification the fact that my mother had never kissed me in her life, had never smiled at me nor spoken in a tone that was the least bit kindly. That she drove me to disastrous complexes, which I overcame only thanks to sport, that she abandoned me to my fate and that, having abandoned me, she tried as best she could to make my life miserable solely on account of a malicious and incomprehensible antipathy toward me. But all this and many even worse things which I don't feel like mentioning would hardly be considered by many as justifying the fact that I accepted the news of my mother's death not only with indifference but even with a certain irritability, for this news blurred for me the only things that were important and essential to me at the time. My mother gave birth to me. She delivered me into the world. And nothing else ought to count at the time of her death. Only this distressing and universal fact, this biological fact, the only one which conciliates the discrepancies between religion and progressive philosophical and social movements. I could expatiate at length that she hadn't in the least delivered me into the world in order to gratify me, but for entirely different reasons, very complicated and having merely an accidental and indirect connection with me. I'd be called not only a monster, but a swine too, and the powerful mythical and biological fact would remain not only unshaken but still more elevated and untouchable. In any case, I had no intention whatsoever of making attacks on that Olympian feeling of holiness. On the contrary. I could feel how, independently of my will, I was giving way to its formal rigors. Inwardly I was indifferent, but outwardly I unthinkingly took on the pose of an orphaned child. Until, glancing in a mirror while washing, I was surprised when I caught sight of my own face. Sorrow, grief, suffering, and many other similar feelings, none of which I felt, were painted there.

The funeral took place two days later. Of course I played the leading part at it. Whereas in the bathroom I could still pull myself together and give my face back its normal expression, at the cemetery this was impossible. I had to look and behave in the way a son behaves at a funeral. The involvement of those attending the ceremony obliged me to. Besides, it would have been difficult suddenly to step forward and explain to everybody that the deceased had been an alien person to me and that even Saint Stanislaus Kostka couldn't have brought himself to find even a scrap of sorrow for such a mother. So I stood with bowed head and a serious expression on my face. My father and the doctor were standing not far from me. Side by side, for the first time since my appearances as a boxer. They had the same expressions as when I hit the floor during a "Dynamo"-Berlin match. I didn't hit the floor from the blow, I merely slipped. This was at the moment when the German gave me a blow on the jaw, which I caught with my arm, but it might have seemed as though it had connected. The German referee saw very well what was what, but slyly took advantage of it and began the count. I won by my opponent giving up in the third round. Dorota was standing with a wrinkled forehead and lips projecting like a beak. From time to time she glanced at me with a look that seemed angry and expressive of solidarity. She had looked at me this way once before, at a meeting in the club when I was threatened with a year's disqualification for allegedly nonproductive criticism of the directorship, and she was first to stand up in my defense. The fellows had brought a wreath with the club ribbons, and Leon Kozak had tears in his eyes. He has a very good mother, whom he loves enormously. For a while I thought I would burst into tears myself. On account of Leon and his mother, of course. Michal Podgorski was elegantly dressed and gloved, like in the photographs of eminent English politicians. I think he's something of a snob, but after all everyone has his weaknesses. I, for instance, don't deny that the company of film stars impresses me a little, but basically I despise them. No. I don't despise them. I don't despise anybody, and contempt seems to me one of the most repulsive feelings. I have noticed and am surely not mistaken in that contempt is characteristic of weak and abject people who are trying to turn attention away from the minor dirty tricks by means of which they struggle through life. Dr. Plucinski was very official and ceremoniously energetic. He seemed to feel very well indeed, and I suppose he must be very fond of funerals. In any case, the center of interest, sympathy, and liking was myself, and I wanted the ceremony to end as soon as possible, because it was becoming harder and harder to bear the role thrust upon me by circumstance and custom. When the coffin was sprinkled with earth, people began coming up to me to offer their condolences. I had the faint hope that they'd consider these due rather to my mother's doctor, but not a bit of it. Besides, he was the first to come up to me. Not, assuredly, in order to throw the responsibility off himself, but on account of inborn modesty and a feeling of tact. My father hammed it up so that I was ashamed to remember afterwards. He smelled of vodka and irritated me so much that I simply wanted to hit him. Purely in theory, of course. By the way, it would have been the last straw if at the funeral of my mother, whom I didn't like and with whom nothing linked me, I had hit my own father. They'd have proclaimed me a degenerate representative of my generation, polemics would have run wild in the literary magazines, and loudest of all would have been those who generally have nothing to say on contemporary matters and lie in wait for just such special occasions; and the opponents of sports, all those programmatic and utterly ideological bunglers, gray and sad people whom I'm basically sorry for, would have jumped for joy.

They all began going away and I remained alone, and wished to remain entirely alone at last. They tactfully sensed this and departed faster and faster. Of course they had no idea what the point really was. I simply wanted to remain alone in order to sigh with relief, remove my mask, and take on my own aspect, and not, as they all thought, to ponder yet awhile over my mother's grave in solitude. In any event I must add that properly speaking it was a sort of comedy played by us all, a collective suggestion summoned up by the tyranny of custom, for after all most of those attending the funeral knew very well that my mother was one of the most profligate of mothers, that nothing tied me to her, and that no one would have the right to condemn me for not having any tender feelings toward her.

Agnieszka hadn't heard about it yet. I never supposed for a moment she would come to the funeral. So much so that I didn't even take the trouble to look furtively around to see whether she was among those present. Furthermore, my formal preoccupation with the rite meant that, although I certainly didn't stop thinking about her entirely, yet my thoughts of her remained somewhere in the background. So it was a shock for me when she suddenly stopped beside me at the moment when the last participants in the funereal ceremony had disappeared around the corner of the little path in the Rakowicki cemetery and I had thought that at last I was alone. She took my hand and for a moment said nothing. This happened just at the moment when I had intended to relax, perhaps to sigh literally with relief. And immediately I had once again to adopt the mourning and orphaned attitude, which I did with the rapidity of a person rushing back to shelter from a storm after he'd gone out into the fresh air, misled by the quiet, and right then a thunderbolt falls not far from him. I felt great joy. Agnieszka was with me. She had come on learning that a misfortune had befallen me. This bore witness to everything and dispelled all my doubts. She didn't know the true state of affairs, but in a difficult moment, not caring about the complicated intrigues proceeding between us, she had hastened to my side. Would it be fitting to admit the truth to her at this moment? Or would it also be fitting to take advantage of the artificially created situation and confirm her affection for me and the concern which wasn't really due to me under the circumstances? It's difficult for me to answer what I considered fitting and what not. Concerning this incident I only know that it became yet another confirmation of the fact that the lack of a consistent attitude in behavior and psychological deceptions only brings very short-term successes. In any case, at the time when Agnieszka was holding my hand in the cemetery I really felt like an unhappy orphaned son, and I felt it for her sake, because she had to participate in all my feelings and I wasn't allowed to disappoint her. And I said quietly, firmly, without looking at her, but only pressing her hand a little more strongly:

"Agnieszka. Here at this moment I promise you. I promise I'll never leave you and that you'll be the last woman in my life."

I didn't even notice I was making the vow over my mother's grave; nothing of the sort would have entered my head, for that would have been as comical as an old-fashioned postcard with the inscription "Congratulations on your birthday," such as Artur Wdowinski collects with relish. It would have been comical and completely irrelevant, even if I had loved and adored my mother to the fullest extent. I made this vow to Agnieszka on account of the old incident with Szymaniak and all its later consequences, and the need for purging and conquering that which seemed suspect and hostile to me in life. It could just as well have happened in a streetcar or a café. However, it occurred in the cemetery. And strangely enough, when I suddenly realized that after all, from a formal point of view, it was a vow taken over my mother's grave, I felt that whether I wanted to or not, whether it struck me as comical or not, this thing placed an additional obligation on me. A vow taken over my mother's grave could only be associated for me in principle with a bad production of a third-rate dramatist of the last century. Besides, when one adds to all this the fact that my mother had hated me as a phenomenon in life, that she really didn't know me at all, and that I didn't know her, the concept "mother" could not mean the same to me that it meant to others. And if one further adds that in general such a thing as a vow can't be treated seriously these days; once in the past it served as a blind for false and deceptive matters and later, like many such matters, it became canonized. Personally I'd abrogate the Olympics vow, and at the last Olympics I had some slight qualms because I started laughing while taking the vow. Well, I couldn't stop myself. After all, the mere fact of taking a vow suggests there's something wrong and that somewhere or other some dirty tricks and confusions are lurking. It ought rather to be passed over in discreet silence, but not be ceremoniously brought to mind. Yet at the cemetery at that time the formal aspect of the accidentally taken "vow over my mother's grave" possessed such an enormous power of a ritual generally sanctified for thousands of years that I couldn't escape from it and yielded to the action of something in which I not only didn't believe, but which I bluntly regarded as comic and trivial.

Agnieszka didn't say anything. She said nothing as we walked toward the exit across the cemetery, holding hands. Not until we reached the street did she speak for the first time:

"What do you intend to do today?"

It was beautiful that she didn't say anything and that her first words concerned everyday and purely mundane matters. It was beautiful, assuming of course that I was suffering and it was necessary to treat me very tactfully, attentively, and with imperceptible concern. But after all I really didn't know now what was genuine and what wasn't. Properly speaking, I knew. Only that which Agnieszka noticed and saw at this moment was genuine. So I really was suffering, I really was the son who'd lost his mother. It was for the sake of Agnieszka that I was he.

When she asked what I intended to do that day, I divined concern and devotion in the question. I understood she was asking me to put her at my service, but she was doing it in a wonderfully tactful way. I felt an enormous joy, unsullied by anything, and it flashed through my head that it was a marvelous coincidence that . . . No, no. There are things which it is utter baseness even to think of fleetingly. No matter what my mother had been, to think that which I wanted to think wasn't permissible, even for a moment. Very fortunately I at once forgot what I'd wanted to think, and only a vague recollection remained that it had been something exceptionally base.

"You know very well, Agnieszka, that I can't imagine anything better than to be with you," I said.

She came closer to me and walked for a time leaning her head lightly on my shoulder. I was furious for not being able to behave normally and display my joy and happiness. At the most I could allow myself some mild sorrow.

Agnieszka suggested coming to me toward evening and preparing supper. She brought a bottle of American whiskey which her uncle Plucinski had sent. The other uncle, from New York. The supper was excellent and Agnieszka went to an enormous amount of trouble to bring me back to stability and turn my thoughts away from the tragedy I had experienced. I could see how happy she felt on realizing that she had fully succeeded and that I was at last starting to laugh sincerely and cordially.

She stayed at my place for a few days and we were very happy together. It was at that time that my apartment was changed beyond recognition. I had a lot of money. My mother's doctor called me to say he wanted to see me. I went to him and he told me unheard-of things. He claimed my mother had loved me very much and altogether had loved the house she left, for she loved my father more than anyone. In fact, it was my father who was unfaithful to my mother, and it was this that she couldn't bear. She had gotten to know the doctor years before, and at first there had been only friendship between them. My mother confided her unhappiness in him, and he consoled her. Then it turned into something deeper. Primarily on his side. For her, he was merely the mainstay of her life (this was how he expressed it) and she assuredly felt great attachment, maybe even something more, toward him. But in truth she loved my father. And me above all else in the world (this was also how he expressed it), and that house of hers.

I received the doctor's account in silence and with a sceptical look on my face. I was wondering why he was telling me this nonsense, assuredly violating his own self-esteem.

He said:

"I see you don't believe too much in what I've told you."

"I can't say I do, particularly."

He lowered his head and rubbed his brow in a manner suggesting he wanted to make an important decision or to recollect something, or else to bring himself to do something that required special courage or was beyond his strength. Apart from this he had an expression on his face which I can only describe as something between resignation and despair. To be sure, apart from what he was dreaming up in his head in connection with me, he was thinking to himself that he was absolutely alone in the world, had nothing to live for, and his life hadn't been a success. He must have loved my mother deeply, and I felt sorry for him. I wanted quite simply to stroke his head and tell him he could count on me, or that henceforward I would be his mainstay, or some other of the things one sometimes says and which one doesn't stick to. But of course I didn't say them, for certain things just don't come through my lips. Agnieszka says I am not a good person. She tells this even to other people. But it assuredly isn't so and she assuredly doesn't believe it herself. But when my mother's doctor rubbed his brow, something gripped me by the throat and I felt a sort of particular solidarity with him. Not especially with him as my mother's doctor, but with him as a person in general. I don't know how to bring this home to myself precisely, just as I don't really know what this solidarity was to have reference to.

He unexpectedly raised his head and looked me straight in the eyes.

"I understand," he said in a clear and determined voice, "that there are circumstances which may possibly entitle you to a certain extent to feel resentment or dislike for your mother."

"I feel neither resentment nor dislike," I said. This was true. I didn't feel anything toward her. Not even this.

Great conviction must have sounded in my voice, for the doctor glanced at me in some surprise and as though taken aback. He gazed at me somehow as though he felt disappointed and had a grudge against me for not feeling any resentment or dislike for my mother. He started rubbing his brow again.

"I understand," he said after long reflection, "you don't want to cause me unhappiness, knowing how very much I loved your mother. And you consider that now, with her gone, it's necessary to forget everything that wasn't good. Or rather, I'd say, everything that might have appeared not good. This approach to the matter speaks well for you; this isn't a surprise to me in the least. You know I always had the highest opinion of you and surely you remember that years ago . . ."

He began leading this certainly difficult conversation in some irrelevant direction but must have suddenly realized this, for he broke off abruptly.

Again he lifted his head and glanced at me boldly, and even with a flash auguring triumph.

"Why talk a lot," he almost shouted, "I have irrefutable proof that your mother loved and remembered you."

He rose, walked energetically up to a landscape painted by Wyspianski and representing a Cracow winter landscape, and moved it aside. Behind the picture was a safe. Hitherto I had seen such things only in movies and I had thought they existed only abroad, or were generally made up. In our own home there must certainly have been a safe concealed behind some picture, but my father probably guarded against revealing it.

In any case, this safe which mother's doctor uncovered behind the Wyspianski picture in his apartment amused me no end. Particularly since it had a little knob, I don't know what it's called, which turns to a prearranged word or combination of numbers. When much later I told Dorota about this safe, she laughed too, but she didn't much believe in it all. In any case, when the doctor turned the knob I chuckled to such an extent that at one moment I couldn't control myself and laughed out loud. But I immediately stifled my laughter by a sort of choking sound which might have given the impression I was restraining my feelings. The doctor certainly thought this, and perhaps even thought I was restraining a sob, for he suddenly stopped turning the knob, as though listening. I simply don't understand why this safe amused me so. The fact is that it amused Dorota just the same, but if I'd asked her why, she too probably wouldn't have been able to answer. It seems to me that the comicality of that safe is something entirely natural, like other comical things, and there's no need to wonder about it.

Finally the doctor finished coping with his satanic mechanism, the little door opened and then he hurriedly brought something out of the interior. At moments he seemed to be reflecting, as though he were sorting something out, finally he turned round, went up to the little table at which we were sitting and placed various strange objects on it. Not, however, that they were at all strange in themselves. Several quite thick bundles of five-hundred-zloty bills, some American dollars, and a little jewelry.

This amused me even more than the safe; perhaps all of it along with the safe, reminiscent of a gangster movie, amused me. But this time I had to control myself. For now he was standing in front of me and gazing into my eyes. His look contained some elements of pathos. He opened his mouth to say something and shut it again. As people do at certain moments not because they're hesitating as to what to say but because they have thought out what it is they're going to say beautifully and are under the pressure of such elevated feelings that they'll be sorry to have it behind them:

"Here," said the doctor finally, "here are the sacred proofs of the attachment your mother, of bright memory, felt for you. Here is the greatest evidence of that care which did not desert her in the moment of her last breath. What you see here is the inheritance she left you. At this moment I am carrying out a duty, I am carrying out her last wish and this . . ."

He was completely spent and had lost the thread. He sat down heavily and started to wipe the sweat from his brow with the back of his hand; then he turned away his face and covered it with one hand.

I felt so abashed that I didn't know what to do with myself. It was essential to extricate myself somehow from this situation, but the doctor seemed turned to stone. The most absurd thoughts came into my head, for example to stroke his head or say:

"Courage, Doctor."

People in American movies often talk to one another in this manner.

Anyway, what was happening was certainly more reminiscent of a movie than of real life, but I must state, based on my own observations, that of late everything that happens between people in life is more reminiscent of a film than of life. By no means because it's so interesting. But because it's so contrived, produced, acted—anyhow, how should I know why? Maybe I'm wrong. After all, the movies have been around a hundred years at the most and people have been hamming it up for a good few thousand years already. Well, yes, but there was always the theater. Admittedly accessible only to a few. For the upper crust. So I think that in former times, only the upper crust hammed it up, but now, thanks to the movies, hamming has become general.

I don't mean to say by all this that the doctor was hamming. Not in the shallow sense of movies at any rate. I watched his acting. This wasn't difficult in any case. He was obviously bamboozling me with all this inheritance. He was anxious to rehabilitate my mother in my memory. He knew very well that she'd behaved basely toward me. This didn't concern me in the least, really. Absolutely not. But it concerned him. It had concerned him during her life and concerned him still more at this time, when it was no longer possible to put matters right. After all, it wouldn't be possible—because what can be set right between two strangers whom nothing links together? Reflecting on all this, I was thinking along the lines of his categories or illusions, or whatever they were. This genuinely noble man, this bungler, this prince of bunglers, really loved my mother. Here I wish to point out that when I call someone a bungler, it doesn't always have to be offensive. Sometimes quite the opposite is true. Sometimes I've thought of bunglers with respect, I envied them, and a sort of longing for bungling settled in me. Who knows but that deep down I didn't belong spiritually to the breed of bunglers, or whether I wasn't potentially a phenomenal specimen of a bungler, something like Tarzan among the monkeys.

The doctor had really loved my mother. It was important to

him to despatch her from this world in a beautiful and dignified manner. On his way to achieving this aim, I was the most important impediment. Someone else, many others, would certainly have tried to remove this impediment in the simplest and most obvious way: they'd have tried to make me out a scoundrel and unnatural son. But this bungler of bunglers had thought up something different. He'd decided to ennoble us both. Her, to whom it could no longer matter, for she was no longer alive, and me to whom it didn't matter because I was still alive. So he was doing this exclusively for his own sake, providing an example by this that sometimes doing something exclusively for one's self may be beautiful, sublime, and noble. As for me, I was behaving like an idiot. In fact, however, I couldn't behave differently. In any case, I didn't know how to.

The doctor was sitting hunched up in his chair. Suddenly he uncovered his face and spoke in a very tired voice. Not only tired but very beseeching:

"Take this inheritance and be on your way."

I gathered it all into my pocket and went out without a word.

Naturally it's possible to accuse me of greed and of cynically taking advantage of the situation. After all, I knew very well that the doctor had invented it all, the money was his, and I had grave doubts even about the jewelry. I'd never in my life seen any of these valuables at my mother's. I was certain he'd given me some family jewelry of his own, and the genuine jewelry left by my mother he was keeping as a souvenir for himself. A most revered souvenir. If I took it all, it wasn't out of greed. In general I wasn't greedy and wasn't concerned about money or so-called material goods. And I definitely was least greedy at precisely this time. This money, dollar bills, and valuables, which were lying before me, were no concern of mine—I didn't feel any link with it. But after all mother's doctor had acted out for himself a great, magnificent, and noble, even most sacred scene, and I couldn't spoil it. Nor butt in with some objection or other, and in this way force myself into the leading role in the drama he'd written for himself. All I could do really was to put everything into my pocket and leave.

Which I did.

At home, I wrapped it all up in a newspaper and placed it in the stove. I don't have a safe. My room has a stove, although there are radiators. Rather, there are radiators although there's a stove. Undoing the little door I deliberately, for devilment, put on a serious expression as though I were opening a safe, but this amused me for only a very short while. I didn't in the least feel disposed to laugh. All this had thrown me off balance, and I was starting to be furious at mother's doctor. I felt somehow as though I'd committed some sort of crime or a particularly dishonorable act. Only now did it begin to enter my head that, properly speaking, the doctor had in a certain sense given me a beating. He'd taken advantage of me for his own inner purposes, admittedly the most sacred though not for me, and now he was undoubtedly sitting there pleased and tranquil. While the bother and distractions were mine.

Agnieszka came soon afterward and I forgot it all.

A few days later I telephoned mother's doctor, tried tactfully to convince him that he ought to take back mother's 'inheritance,' that it didn't mean anything to me, even if it had been her intention to pass them on to me. He was shocked and started talking about the most holy wish of the dead woman and such various things. He was firm and I was able to convince myself that he hadn't made this gesture on the impulse of the moment, but had thought it out well. There wasn't any help for it.

The inheritance was lying in the stove and I didn't mean to touch it. Sometimes I thought to myself that it would be best if someone lit the stove without knowing about it. Once I even said perfunctorily to Agnieszka that it was chilly in the apartment and the radiators were heating badly. Although she didn't yet live exclusively at my place, she had a key to the apartment and sometimes liked to prepare various domestic surprises for me. However, she said that I must be dreaming, for the radiators heated like the devil and she'd even had to turn them down.

Then once the collector from the electric company came; I didn't have any money in the house and took a five-hundred-zloty bill out of the stove. Thus it somehow started and when something begins, everyone knows what follows. I wanted to give Agnieszka the jewelry, but she refused it. She took only one brooch and wore it. I gave the emerald earrings to Dorota. She looked fine in earrings. Agnieszka once saw her in these earrings. From that moment on she no longer liked her.

Later I learned that the doctor had married his assistant from the clinic. Apparently he'd been having an affair with her for at least five years.

All the same, he went to my mother's grave every Sunday. That was a fact.

One day I realized that all this with Agnieszka was also a mistake. I wasn't really certain whether it could be described thus.

Because I couldn't in any event include Agnieszka under the heading unsuccessful affairs with girls, disillusions in love, or anything like that. I was tied to Agnieszka. I was very strongly tied. Not only by the vow over my mother's grave. A vow I had to keep. Quite apart from this I felt very strongly tied to her. I didn't really know by what. By my honor, my life's challenge which at any price I had to carry out to the end. But it was in a certain way a solemn and, so to say, sublime attachment. Other attachments also existed, without which, perhaps, the solemn and sublime one would lose value. For there existed an everyday attachment. Who knows but what such an attachment is not stronger than the most startling insanities of love. Various startling insanities have the property of being inclined, for no reason, to pass by and leave no trace behind. But an everyday attachment is an obstinate, constant, harassing thing. It wasn't the same with Agnieszka that it had been with other girls. Maybe because she had a vital predominance over me and made me feel this. Quite simply, I was afraid of her. I don't know why, but I was afraid of her. I considered her an authority. Purely formally, of course. From fear or maybe for the sake of peace and quiet. Which in the end came out the same. No. It wasn't entirely so. I recognized her formally as an authority, while basically despising her judgment and opinions, in order somehow to reward her, to conceal not only from her and our circle but also from myself the fact that I didn't love her. Because despite the fact that I irritated her at every step, that she despised me as an athlete and that properly speaking she couldn't stand me, I knew that after all she loved me. This was precisely the worst. There was no way of wriggling out of it. Were it not for that, obviously, I'd be liberated from my vow and all the other decisions. I'd be able to seek out for myself another object for carrying on the honorable showdown with life and giving satisfaction for the dirty tricks I'd played. Would I be able to? I even had to. But under these circumstances, what could be done? Agnieszka loved me. She'd become involved through me in something against which she was clearly guarding herself. In something which didn't suit her at all, but from which she didn't know how to seek shelter. She felt resentment and hostility toward me because she loved an athlete who was a great deal below her as far as intellect was concerned. Because of this, she was trying to recoup her losses on me and humiliating me at every step, but she couldn't stop loving me, because it had somehow worked out so catastrophically. Catastrophically both for her and for me.

She was largely to blame in this. She was deceiving me. Then, at the start, she wasn't herself. She was trying to please me and with the devilish intuition of the situation which women often manage to get, she would play the part of someone entirely different. A sort of girl from Hemingway's novels, someone I imagined to myself, for whom I yearned but whom I'd never met. Most probably she'd imitated Jowita. For Agnieszka wasn't Jowita. Fortunately. For a long time I was certain she'd betray me. Until I realized that Jowita really existed and was someone else entirely. I was certain I'd never see her again in my life. But it would have been terrible if she hadn't existed. That is to say if she'd been an invention and trick of Agnieszka's. Because properly speaking I loved Agnieszka as Jowita. When I stopped loving her, I also stopped, obviously, loving Jowita. She was fading, she was disappearing in my imagination and on that account I felt despair and emptiness. But when I knew she really existed, the thought of her gave me encouragement. Jowita stood above everything. She was the ideal of a woman and of womanhood. An ideal unattainable by me, but existing. Because of this it was irrelevant that in some strange way I loved Helena. Helena was Helena, but Jowita was Jowita. Well, there's no better way of explaining this.

It turned out that Agnieszka wasn't Jowita. Not only literally but also metaphorically. As soon as she considered the introductory period ended, she revealed her true features. Here I don't have anything bad in mind by saying her true features. Such an expression is generally used in political articles when it is intended to demonstrate maliciously that some opponent or other is a depraved scoundrel. Agnieszka had a certain disposition, which in itself was perhaps worthy of recognition, but which simply didn't suit me. She was terribly matter-of-fact and scrupulous. A true know-it-all. She had tremendous intellectual self-esteem and in general a vital self-esteem. Without a moment of interruption she kept striving to gratify this self-esteem, and it seemed that she simply had no time for anything else. Such a character might please Michal Podgorski for example. Moreover he did like it, though it didn't seem to me that he was interested in Agnieszka as a woman. It might please Michal Podgorski, but for me it was something alien. The worst of it was that Agnieszka considered that since she'd shown her true features, then I too ought to reveal my own true features, corresponding to hers. But she didn't take into consideration that from the beginning I'd been operating exclusively with my genuine features and didn't have any others. For this reason she felt disappointed and cheated. She kept trying to knock at my door, as it were, or at my window, for me to open up and show my expected features. Hence the constant conflicts and misunderstandings between us.

She was everlastingly trying to lead me onto the right path, to change me, to educate me, and she couldn't get over the fact that I was an athlete, not an intellectual, and that in the literary weeklies, if I read them at all, I preferred to read the amusing articles rather than the serious essays.

After my mother's funeral Agnieszka set up house with me and it seemed she'd stay for good.

Those were really beautiful days. Surely some of the most beautiful in my generally uninteresting life. Afterwards it was hard for me to evaluate them. One evening, as we were eating supper, I began to yield in horror to the impression that I was bored. I wanted to go out somewhere, meet Artur Wdowinski or go to a movie with Dorota. Agnieszka complained of a headache and was silent. But this wasn't why I felt bored. It originated with me, not with her. The next day she went out early to the Academy and in the evening telephoned that she had some unexpected work and would have to spend the night with a girl friend. I pretended I was disappointed by this, but basically I was relieved. This alarmed me even more than the previous evening's feeling of boredom, and I started to reflect how it would all work out.

Agnieszka didn't come back to me. That is, she didn't come back to my apartment for good. For everything had been leading up to her bringing her things and our living together. But in certain matters Agnieszka had great sensitivity for her situation, even though in others she startled me outright by her callousness. At that time she knew it was too early to stay with me for good, and skillfully withdrew. Properly speaking, nothing changed through this. She kept the keys and when she came to me, she adopted the role of housewife with the greatest ease. But the fact that we were living apart demanded some sort of comment, some sort of official version. And this too Agnieszka settled expertly. She told me:

"You know what . . . You have to understand certain things. It's obviously absurd, this keeping up appearances. But it's a question of my family. They're bourgeois know-it-all blockheads. Do you know what bourgeois know-it-all blockheads are? You see! You don't. I'll tell you. For them it would be quite a blow if we were to live together without being married. But I have to reckon with them. Well, I simply don't have the strength to cause them any unpleasantness and disappointment."

So I started to persuade Agnieszka that we should get married as soon as possible. And here Agnieszka proved to be marvelously

inconsistent. She laughed at me for being a stick-in-the-mud and
for yielding to the terrorism of artificial customs.

"If you're ashamed to be living with me on intimate terms," she
said, "then we can break it off. I'll even forgive you if you don't
say hello when we meet, for I'll understand I'm compromising
you. You're sometimes really amazingly backward. How can such
matters be a problem in general to anyone in the second half of
the twentieth century?"

I still liked this Agnieszka greatly. Everything that bore witness
to her femininity pleased me. For what is more feminine than the
uttering within a few seconds of two completely contradictory
opinions?

But Agnieszka revealed her feminine traits less and less often.
She was wise, sensible, preoccupied with striving for professional
perfection and, in addition to this, somehow terribly artificial.
Artificial, I think, in the sense of a planned intellectual attitude.
This plan included me, unfortunately. The fact that she arranged
my apartment prettily was of course positive. On the negative side
was that at every step she tried to elevate me intellectually. To
her level. I strongly suspect that basically she was guided in this
not by a concern to improve my value, but by giving both me and
our circle to understand how much lower than she I stood. This
was of course one of the ways of attaching me to her and making
me dependent. An undoubtedly good and effective way. I felt dependent on Agnieszka and became increasingly attached to her.
This arranging of matters between a man and a woman, so that a
certain kind of attachment is accompanied by an inversely pro-
portional strength of desire for other women is particularly satanic
on the part of nature. I was growing more and more powerfully
tied to Agnieszka. But the more strongly I grew attached and the
more clearly I saw how much she loved me, the more despair
seized me that various areas of the charms of life were becoming
closed to me once and for all. That stupid vow was closing them,
and there wasn't any help for it.

Although we didn't live together, Agnieszka and I were a typical married couple. But she arrogated rights over me more tyran-
nical than the most stanch and legal wife, and I submitted to
them with greater deference than the most typical husband of
many years' standing. I met Agnieszka's parents. They were
cheerful, liberal people without prejudices. Before the war, the father had been an engineer in the Cegielski factory, and after the
war he established an automobile workshop in Poznan. She came
from the landed gentry. In her own day she'd entered into a mis-

alliance of a sort. But all the landed gentry relatives of the Plucinskis were rather rebellious; uncle Plucinski even belonged to the Polish Socialist Party. The other uncle, the American one, had run away from home as a boy, stowed away to the United States, and made himself a respectable fortune. In any case, it was out of the question that Agnieszka's parents might be outraged by our living together unmarried. She'd invented that. We decided we'd marry after her return from the United States. She already had a passport, visa, and everything. She could leave at any time. She kept setting dates and then postponing them. I knew why, but I couldn't refer to it with her in direct conversation. Agnieszka was scared of what might happen during her absence. She was scared to part with me. She knew how dangerous it was. And she was right. That is, she'd have been right, were it not for the vow. I was attached to Agnieszka to the end of my life. She could go tranquilly wherever she wanted and for as long as she wanted. Now nothing could change between us.

At the start of my athletic career, I'd entered the National steeplechase. This was my first race. From the very beginning I broke into the lead and quickly bypassed all opponents. But I lost my way and got off the track. I noticed it and turned back to the designated course at the same place where I'd left it. I lost at least two kilometers. Despite this, I caught up with my opponents and won. I didn't really win, because they disqualified me. I recalled this incident very often later on. I recalled it also in connection with Agnieszka. I didn't know why. If I'd reflected more profoundly, maybe I'd have happened on the reason. But I didn't feel like it. It was enough that I could sense the link between what was happening in my life and what happened in my struggles on the racetrack. That consoled me. Why? I didn't know that either. It isn't at all good to know too much. Agnieszka wanted to know everything and wanted to be guided by intellect alone. Well and what would have happened to her if she had found out how it really was between us? What would have happened to her if she'd known what was going on between Helena and me?

But what was going on, properly speaking?

Formally speaking, nothing was happening that could be regarded as bad. Formally! Pah! How many dirty tricks happen because they've invented the concept of a formal aspect of incidents.

For if nothing bad was happening formally, then why couldn't I look Ksiezak in the eye? Why did I avoid him and try with refined baseness to keep seeking pretexts for misunderstandings with him? Formal pretexts, not connected with what was essen-

tial. And why did I behave in a similar way with Agnieszka? In
any case, it was very easy to invent formal pretexts for misunderstandings with her. I couldn't complain that she made my task
difficult. It was another matter with Ksiezak. But why was he
such an ass? Why didn't he see anything of what was going on
around him, around us? After all, he ought to have guessed something, or at least sensed something, that time he telephoned from
Warsaw. With such a marvelous, noble character, he'd have been
able to settle the matter subtly and imperceptibly. So here I'd
reached the depths of baseness! I bore a grudge against a man
whom I might at any moment betray and cheat. To whom, properly speaking, I'd already done just that. If I were to give up making use of the formal aspect of the problem. I bore a grudge
against him because he'd done nothing to interfere with me.

In reality he'd done nothing to interfere; in fact he'd done
much to help. But it wasn't his fault. But was it mine? How long is
it possible to suffer the torment of renunciation, taking into consideration that an isolated person defends himself against fully
mobilized nature, equipped with the most dynamic thermonuclear weapon?

I suffered indescribable torment when, on returning from Helena, I threw myself on the couch and tried to grasp the meaning
of what had happened. I suffered physical torments—I wanted
Helena so much. In all my life I never wanted anything so much
as I wanted her. But this was still nothing in comparison with
what happened later.

It was very lucky that Agnieszka was away. She'd gone to Warsaw to take care of some additional formalities in connection with
leaving for America. Though I think she didn't really have anything to take care of. She was using this as a means to postpone
her departure. She'd already received her diploma and had no
reasons for waiting any longer. I pretended to believe that nothing
was ready because I simply wanted her to go to Warsaw for a few
days at least. I had to have some respite from her. And because
Michal Podgorski was going to Warsaw by car just then, I asked
him to take her along and somehow I skillfully got everything into
a muddle so that however much she wanted to wriggle out of it,
she couldn't. But she wanted to very much. As though she sensed
that nothing good would happen during her absence. She had a
cross and pouting expression when she entered the car, looked at
me angrily and was even slightly impolite to Michal who, innocent as a babe, couldn't guess that it was on my account. Of
course it was pure coincidence that both Agnieszka and Ksiezak

left at the same time. But in the end, everything that happens, happens as a result of more or less obvious coincidences. Only writers have a great fear of coincidences, for they fear that they lower the value of literature. Remarque wrote something on this subject in his *Arch of Triumph*. I'm repeating after him. I liked that writer very much. Agnieszka spoke of him scornfully.

So I suffered awfully on that couch. Had I been in a state to think of anything other than Helena, I'd probably have thought that it was an intolerable thing for me to suffer on this couch, on which not so long ago I'd suffered similarly on account of Agnieszka. Maybe similarly, as I didn't remember too much of the nature of that other suffering. But I thought of this only later and at that time, if I thought of Agnieszka at all, it was only to sigh with relief that she'd gone to Warsaw and there was no likelihood of her suddenly appearing here.

I was suffering physically. My body was burning, my fingernails being torn out, my eyes scratched out. But this was nothing in comparison with what happened afterward.

At that time I managed to control myself sufficiently not to call Helena or go back to her. This was probably one of the most unusual achievements in my life. Worn out by torture, I fell asleep fully dressed. Generally speaking, I've heard that people who are tormented spend sleepless nights. I don't know why, but with me it was just the opposite. Never did I sleep so well and soundly as when I had serious anxieties or when something made me particularly uneasy.

I woke up next morning and at once wondered what would have happened if Agnieszka had suddenly come in and seen me asleep with my clothes on. As she usually did, she'd have said with regret, barely concealing her deep satisfaction:

"I'm very sorry, it's my fault. I forgot to inform you that the development of civilization invented pyjamas and that the period when man, covered with skins, used to sleep on a makeshift bed of leaves, is already behind us. It seems to me, darling, that in general the couch is too complicated an object for you, and surely it will be enough if you sleep on the doormat."

She'd have been so happy to be thus able to inform me that I'm an uncultured person and that an enormous difference in standards separated me from her, that she wouldn't even wonder why I was really sleeping in my clothes; she wouldn't have thought it was somewhat suspicious.

I rapidly undressed, jumped into the tub and thought all the time what a cutting reply I'd have given Agnieszka. Not for some time did I remember Helena and everything I'd lived through the previous day. I wanted to laugh, but simultaneously I felt ashamed. Exactly the sort of shame I'd have felt if what hadn't happened had happened, and as though I were regretting it.

"It's terrible," I thought, "that a person undergoes momentary illusions which, despite their temporary nature, are so powerful that they have the strength to change the course of his fate. The illusion of thermonuclear power bursts and vanishes, but altered fate remains. To the devil with it all. What luck that I managed to control myself yesterday."

At this moment the thought of Helena did not arouse any feelings in me. None apart from a sort of mixture of distaste and shame. This mixture covered something dangerous, but I pretended not to notice.

I went to the office. There I learned that Michal Podgorski had called from Warsaw. He wasn't coming back until next day and asked me to see to it that the workshop completed a job for the Mining Academy which we'd put off for a month. I was disappointed because I thought that Agnieszka too would not be coming back today. It would be more convenient for her to come back by car with Michal. But I very much wanted Agnieszka to be with me. I felt affection for her and thought that when all was said and done, she was the person closest to me in the whole world. I came to the conclusion that in general I had a wrong attitude toward her and must change it for her sake.

As I was returning home, still on the stairs, I heard the phone ringing and ran up the stairs so as to be in time to take the call.

I opened the door so violently that a reproduction of Manet's *Olympia* flew off the wall. I'd noticed long ago that it was hanging in the wrong place, too near the front door. I'd foreseen that sooner or later it would be knocked off by the door. But I hadn't felt like rehanging it and kept putting it off. Agnieszka never said anything about it. She didn't know what attitude to take toward the impressionists. They were already not contemporary enough for her, but still insufficiently classical. She therefore pretended that she just didn't notice the reproduction of *Olympia*. This was very characteristic of Agnieszka.

Running into the room, I slipped and bumped into a little table on which a vase was standing. I managed to grab it in the air and fell on the telephone holding it like a relay stick. I never ran in a relay race in my life, but I would very much like to. Unfortunately, relay races aren't run over my distances.

I lifted the receiver and for a moment I said nothing. I was out of breath and ashamed to say "hello" in a broken voice. I wanted my voice to sound rather easy and even nonchalant. I waited for my breathing to level out. Sometimes I run five thousand meters and can breathe as evenly as though I'd woken up a moment ago. But here, running a few yards to this telephone, I'd lost my breath.

"What's going on there?" after a moment I heard an irritated voice in the receiver. It was Ksiezak's voice. "Is anybody there?"

"I'm here," I said.

"So why the devil don't you speak? Playing hide-and-seek, or something?"

"I answered," I told him, "only something in my phone keeps breaking down. The wire is cut off somewhere."

I was lying to him. Why was I lying to him? Why was I trying to hide from him that I was out of breath?

"Listen to me . . . are you listening now? Answer, do you hear?"

"I'm listening, I'm listening. You don't have to shout, that won't help."

Already then I was beginning to be mad at him, but what was more disgusting, I sought justification for my anger in lying about the phone being out of order.

"What are you so mad for?" asked Ksiezak with the particular pathos of someone who, hurrying to someone with a store of interesting news meets with indifference and lack of interest. "Why are you mad? Maybe I interrupted your work?"

I felt sorry.

"No, no, Edward. Forgive me if it seemed that I'm mad at you. This telephone upsets me."

Lying about the telephone was becoming universal. It served not only for attack but also for defense.

"So listen. I've many interesting things to tell you. I got around a bit in Warsaw. You know what? It seems to me we shall succeed in putting through some of the things we talked about. I've written a memo and the point is to submit it at a general meeting."

I was playing with the little vase. I threw it high up and caught it down near the floor. At the last moment. I wasn't interested in the general meeting, or Ksiezak's memo, or what he'd been doing there. I knew these things by heart already.

Why had I hurried to the phone so? Why did I get so out of breath? I'd almost demolished the apartment. *Olympia* was lying naked on the floor in the passage. Naked amidst broken glass. This association seemed unpleasant to me. I bore a grudge against

Ksiezak. After all, it was he ringing when I ran so hard for the phone. He was chattering on about what he'd done in Warsaw. I wasn't listening. I was wondering what Helena was doing at this time. Was she home?

I had a long cord on the telephone and could walk around the entire apartment, talking. I put down the little vase, took the telephone, walked into the hallway and picked *Olympia* up off the floor. I examined her. I felt relieved to have extricated her from the glass. Was Helena home or not? And if she wasn't home, where was she? Suddenly I felt the blood rush to my head. The nudity of Olympia was associated with Helena for me. It was a peculiar feeling. I'm really not an erotomaniac and pornography doesn't interest me. But if in the association of Olympia's nakedness with Helena there was something that might seem pornographic, then it was assuredly pornography of a higher order, idealistic pornography, so to say. Not that physical nudity was associated directly for me with the possible nudity of Helena, but the concept of nakedness with Helena in general, completely independent of whether she were clothed or not. The concept of nakedness as a form of liberation and joy. Of course, it's easy to analyze all this and supply commentaries later. At that time the decisive fact was that I associated the nakedness of Olympia with Helena and that as a result of this, I experienced a rush of blood to the head. I was far from seeking the origin and essence of this phenomenon. I was more interested in whether Helena was at home and, if so, whether she knew Ksiezak was talking to me and what she thought about that. I didn't listen to any of his chattering and at that moment I didn't even feel embarrassed by the fact that I was thinking about Helena, and in such a manner, and this moreover at a moment when he, unaware of anything, was making me friendly confidences. By the way, Ksiezak's chatter never interested me. It was a strange business with him. He was certainly an excellent trainer and I owed him a lot. If not everything. On the track he was resilient, precise, and definite. But away from the track he had his own particular notions of reforming and organizing, ill-judged and impractical. This was his weakness, which everybody treated with forbearance. It consisted mainly in that he magnified a simple and trivial matter into universal and basic dimensions. Just as though he'd built a sort of electric brain for the purpose of opening a pack of cigarettes. He didn't always yield to this, but had such attacks from time to time. He wrote memos that nobody read, called meetings to which hardly anyone went, took everyone aside and prevailed upon them in matters that were of no use to anyone and didn't interest anybody. Then these matters melted away into the air and Ksiezak, as if he didn't notice, set up new ones with enthusiasm and fervor. This tendency of his must have been the result of various disappointments in his life, and it constituted an attempt to compensate. Ksiezak had artistic leanings, he dreamed of becoming a pianist, but he lacked the talent. He wanted to substitute sports for it. In sprinting he had attained only mediocre results. Here too the talent to raise him above the average was lacking. Then it wasn't enough for him that he really was a fine trainer, that our sports owed him much and could be proud of him. He was left with an unfulfilled longing from sports and the stage for individual stunts; hence this boring people with long and woolly speeches at meetings and the writing of verbose, incomprehensible memos. And yet at the same time, where definite sporting matters were concerned no one could solve a problem as correctly, compactly and quickly as he. The worst of it was that he'd picked on precisely me for his trusted ally. Admittedly this concerned the good, concrete matters as well as the idiotic ones, but this distinction didn't suit me at all. For in general it didn't suit me to have Ksiezak single me out. I alone was on first-name terms and on an equal footing with him, and he considered me something better than the rest. I wasn't at all sure whether this wasn't because I came from what's called a "good home." The guys in our club mostly came from "poor homes," with the exception of Komorowski, the bowler. But then he'd been in the Soviet Union during the war. It was stupidity on Ksiezak's part to single me out on account of that "good home." If only he'd known what sort of a home it was and what it had led me to. If only he knew how very much I wanted to be from a "poor home" or have spent the war years in the Soviet Union. In any case, Ksiezak's attitude toward me singled me out from the other guys in the club in a way that was scarcely desired by me. What mattered to me was not to differ from them in anything. Maybe then I'd reach some sort of balance? But by accommodating Ksiezak I'd reached a point where something divided me from those men whom I liked so very much, whom I envied because they were what they were, and whom, after all, in the depths of my soul I treated somewhat contemptuously.

"Are you listening to what I'm saying?"

"Yes, I'm listening, I'm listening. Why shouldn't I be listening?"

"I thought it was the wire again."

"No, the wire is OK."

"Well, what? Can you find a minute for me?"

"Naturally. You know my time is always at your disposal."

"Above all, I know I can always count on you. I'll send you Helena right away."

"What?"

"Can you hear me or not? Get that phone repaired, the devil take it. It's impossible to talk naturally with you."

"What?"

"Can't you hear me?"

"Listen . . . not very well."

"Hello?"

"Yes, yes. Well, go on."

"So I'll send Helena to you right away with this memo. Can you hear?"

"Yes, I can hear you. For God's sake don't keep asking whether I can hear, just talk."

"And I beg you to look through it today, make your comments, and send them to me. Helena will bring it to you, and then come back for it. I'd like to send it to Warsaw early tomorrow morning. You know, it's a question of their reading it before the general meeting. You know?"

"Yes, yes."

"What, yes, yes?"

"Well, to get there before the general meeting."

"You're the only one who understands the importance of these matters."

Whereas earlier the blood had rushed to my head, now at this moment I could feel a powerful wave of heat course through all my body. I was still holding *Olympia*. I glanced at her and hurled her into the depths of the room.

"Well, what, Marek? Settled?"

"Listen, Edward . . . I wanted to tell you that . . ."

"What? Speak up. Now I can't hear."

"Listen, Edward. I'll very gladly do it, naturally. But why trouble Helena. As it is, I have to take care of something in your neighborhood. I'll drop by . . ."

"Too late, Helena already left. She undertook to do it gladly. She even offered, so don't hesitate. She said she wanted to make up to herself for behaving so stupidly yesterday. She's on her way —she'll be there right away. As it is, you'd pass one another."

So I had the answer to where Helena was and what she was doing.

"Then you know what, Edward . . . Maybe . . ."

"Marek, excuse me, there's someone at the door. Listen, so long. Thank you in advance."

He hung up. I held the receiver to my ear for a while longer. I was standing in the hallway with the phone in my hand, on the broken glass. Then I went slowly back into the room. I put the telephone on the little table by the couch and stared at the window for a while with a feeling of terrible fatigue. The waves of heat which had seemed to quiet down, began flowing with increasing strength. In a little while Helena would be in this room. Suddenly my whole apartment seemed as naked as Olympia. And as Leda, which I now recollected. Soon Helena would be here and supernatural, mythological, and Olympian laws would begin to rule. I felt pressure in the pit of my stomach. It seized me with ferocious joy. Very likely Pan experienced something of the sort while chasing driads, since we're on mythology. I knew that when Helena crossed the threshold of this apartment, nothing would be of any help.

She was coming here to me. I pictured her to myself in the tight red pants and black golf sweater amidst *my* furniture and *my* objects of daily use and everything was terrifyingly naked, and Helena was the most naked in those accursed pants and the accursed sweater, which was also, to tell the truth, very tight. I ran into the kitchen and grabbed the brush and dustpan. I was alarmed to find how much my hands were trembling. But that was only for a moment, for all feelings other than the completely indescribable desire for Helena lost access to me. The brush and dustpan were very nice. Nylon, moldy green in color. One day Agnieszka brought them from a commission store and at the same time ostentatiously threw my old and really soiled brush and pan into the trash can. Of course she didn't let the opportunity slip of calling me a disgusting slob and accursed sloven. She tried whenever she could to make me feel her superiority, and I didn't understand too well why that should really be necessary to her. I suspected that basically she gloried in the fact that her family on her mother's side came from the landed gentry, though of course she'd never have admitted to anything of the sort. In any case, I swear she considered that as far as origins were concerned she was highly superior to me, who am descended from Cracow philistines. It's really funny that I should have to discuss this topic at all. But, since I'm mentioning it, although it's a fact that the parents of my mother had a hat shop on Slawkowska Street, it's also a fact that the Arenses descended from Swedish gentry. What of it if after the conquests of Gustav Adolph they remained permanently in Poland and went very much to pot? It's really funny to mention anything on this topic. But it was Agnieszka who kept forcing me to make a fool of myself. In any case at that time when my hands trembled, when waves of heat flowed over me time and again and there was a pressing in the pit of my stomach, I didn't for a moment think that Agnieszka had bought this brush and dustpan for me; quite generally speaking I didn't for a moment think that, after all, this was our shared apartment, in which we'd experienced beautiful, happy times and which, come what might, I ought to respect. Not likely! I thought of this only later; and only later was I ashamed of myself. Now this apartment was no-body's. Above all not Leda's and Olympia's. I hastily swept up the glass in the hallway, and this physical process of clearing away sobered me a little. I thought to myself that I could run away if I felt like it. I could go out of the house and meet Helena in the street. At the very moment this thought came to me, the doorbell rang.

I froze. I was still crouching on the floor. I was holding the moldy, green brush and matching pan. I started to move toward the kitchen on my knees. I was not only concerned with getting rid of the brush and pan. I obviously couldn't open the door while holding these objects in my hand, for that would not suit the sit-uation, no matter how things went afterwards. But it wasn't only a question of that. After all, I had to adopt some sort of attitude and some kind of facial expression too. I didn't yet know precisely what kind, but in any event not like the facial expression of a man who a moment ago was sweeping broken glass into a dustpan. I suddenly realized what terrible deception all this was. For after all I was concerned with making an unusual impression on Hel-ena. In a moment I'd open the door. Cool, controlled, very mas-culine. She'd be standing in front of me in her tight red pants and black golf sweater, she'd have to yield to the charm of my cool, masculine control. I was mobilizing all methods and means of summoning up this effect in a moment, although at the same time I was determined to act forbiddingly and not even let Helena into the apartment, but to take Ksiezak's memo from her at the door. But it wasn't this which was surely the most fraudulent of all. At that moment we were no more than a yard, at the most a yard and a half, away from one another. I could almost hear and in fact did hear her breathing. We were so close to one another, but the door separated us and we couldn't see one another. And meanwhile I, who was to be so uncommon in a moment, so very masculine and so specifically attractive and forbidding, was creeping on my knees with the brush and dustpan, symbolic of something most comical, pitiable, and pathetic. Maybe she too, who in a moment was to confront me as the most uncommon woman in the world, was making stupid preparatory faces, without which nobody is accustomed to appearing in public and which are something much more intimate than the most intimate and shameful physiological functions.

Anyway, these reflections didn't enter my head then. Only later did I properly evaluate that crawling into the kitchen on my knees. At the time I was so very preoccupied with the necessity of adopting a masculine and unusual attitude, that I attributed it to myself even in this pitiable and grotesque crawling on all fours.

When I finally reached the kitchen, I rose, tipped the glass into the bucket and put the brush and pan back in their place. For a moment I reflected. The devil alone knows what about. And yet I had to reflect about something, because I suddenly felt the decisive willpower and unbeatable strength to come to terms with even the most treacherous charm which the figure in tight red pants and black golf sweater would exert over me.

With a determined step, not doubting my victory, I went to the door and opened it.

I don't understand why I had imagined to myself with such particular stubbornness that Helena would be dressed in the tight red pants and black golf sweater. This was proof that I'd lost all common sense and self-control. She appeared in such attire only at home and in general it was unthinkable that she'd be bold enough to cross Cracow wearing it. I wasn't in a fit state at that moment to picture her otherwise and had insisted exclusively on such an appearance. It's possible that had she actually appeared in that form at my door I'd have succeeded in what I was planning.

I'd intended to say politely though coolly:

"Thank you for taking the trouble and excuse my not asking you in, but there's a terrible mess. I'll send it back to Edward myself. Goodbye."

I'd have taken from her that accursed, idiotic memo and quickly shut the door. Maybe immediately afterwards I'd have howled with despair and maybe even fainted. But I'd have done it. For sure.

Meanwhile, when I opened the door, I saw something I not only hadn't expected, but which I couldn't even imagine. In front of me Helena was standing, or properly speaking not Helena but a being halfway between a Saxon porcelain figurine and Brigitte

Bardot. Only in the sense of attire, for in general Helena wasn't like Brigitte Bardot or anything of that sort. In contrast to Dorota and even to a certain degree to Agnieszka, Helena had nothing girlish about her. Helena was a woman. She was a mature, marvelous woman. A mature woman was standing in front of me in the dress of a girl wanting to be taken for a woman. She had a wide blue skirt, probably with a petticoat. The neckline of her blouse was very low-cut and held tight by something like lace. On her head a wide straw hat with a blue ribbon. She held a parasol, also very lacy, like a petticoat. Somehow it was very improper. She was all somehow lacy and smiling like a child.

"Helena," I said quietly, or perhaps I didn't say it, it merely seemed so to me. In any case I didn't say what I had thought up and I even forgot that I was to say something of the sort.

She stood and smiled, and I felt I was growing faint; I remembered that formerly I had derided the description of someone fainting for love and claimed that such a thing is impossible in practice. It seemed to me that I would instantly throw myself at her and seize her in my arms and wouldn't even have the strength to draw her into the room and that we'd remain clasped in an embrace on the stairs.

But then she said calmly and matter-of-factly:

"What's this? Aren't you going to ask me in?"

Sometimes it happens in the ring that one receives a powerful blow after which one loses consciousness and then one gets another blow which somehow hits so strangely that consciousness comes back.

This remark of Helena's was precisely such a blow, after the first one I'd received on opening the door.

"Yes . . . Of course. Please come in."

"I've come to leave you this scribbling of Edward's," said Helena, entering. "Does it make any sense?"

"No. It doesn't make sense. It doesn't make any sense at all."

"Tell me, why does he make a fool of himself? After all, he's such an intelligent man. Everyone laughs at him on account of these memos."

I didn't reply. I was really thinking that the question related to her coming. I suddenly felt stupid. I felt a mortal chill in me. Helena was calm and matter-of-fact. Maybe she really came only because Ksiezak asked her to and nothing was hidden behind this? Maybe everything that had happened yesterday hadn't happened at all, but only seemed so to me.

She threw a cardboard folder on the table, made a gesture as though she wanted to sit down in an armchair, but hesitated.

She glanced at me.

"I wanted to sit down," she said, "but I have the impression you're not delighted with my visit. It doesn't seem to me that you want to keep me. Did I interrupt you in anything?"

She didn't wait for a reply and immediately added:

"So I'll be going."

I was standing in the center of the room. I didn't say anything. Helena waited a moment, and then laughed. She laughed in a very particular way, threw her parasol on the table by the folder and sat down in the armchair.

I already knew that I hadn't imagined anything of what happened yesterday, but that what had happened had really happened. The chill began giving way and in turn a powerful warmth flooded me. Helena is in my room. She has come to me. She's here, and I can do what I like with her. I even must do what I like. Nothing will save me from that, just as nothing will save me from becoming finally once and for all a scoundrel. I felt a great desire, even a sacred desire as Mother's doctor would have said, of avoiding that, of not losing my self-esteem and of keeping all vows and decisions. What's to be done when desire in the opposite direction was no less great or even, I'd say, in a sense no less sacred.

"You're almost throwing me out," said Helena, "but I'm staying. See what women are like?"

"Helena," I said quietly and redundantly, "you didn't understand me right. What Edward writes makes sense. It really makes sense. And nobody laughs at him."

Helena made a gesture as though she wanted to tell me not to bother her head with matters that didn't concern her.

"Do you know women at all?" she asked. And without waiting for a reply she went on: "For it seems to me you don't know women. You're very intelligent, but you don't know women. And that isn't good for you. In life, you're going to have a lot of worries on account of women. Because you don't know them. I'm telling you, I could help you a great deal. Do you know that? If you trusted me, I could help you a great deal. But I know you don't trust me. Too bad . . ."

She stopped. I saw she'd suddenly lost her self-assurance and the impudence she'd artificially strived for had deserted her.

"I'll be going," she said in a weary voice, and she rose.

"No, no. Don't go," I cried.

I hadn't intended to say that. I myself don't know how it came about that I said it. She glanced at me with a smile which made my head reel. She picked up the parasol from the table. It seemed to me she'd regained her self-assurance.

"Don't think badly of me," she said, "you mustn't think badly of me. You ought rather to try and understand me. No one in my life has understood me yet. I should like you to be able to understand me. I really like you very much, Marek, although you always sulked at me and thought badly of me."

"I never thought badly of you."

I said this without conviction but only because I realized that what Helena was saying had no significance. That she was speaking in order to speak, just as I was replying in order to reply, for we both feared the silence that might suddenly fall between us.

"You've always thought badly of me," said Helena, "you're denying it unnecessarily."

She bent down and picked up *Olympia* from the floor, where I'd previously thrown it. She examined it attentively and smiled to herself.

"Put that down," I shouted.

She glanced at me in surprise.

"Please put it down," I repeated more calmly. This time almost imploringly.

Helena shrugged and threw *Olympia* down on the floor again.

"You don't like me," she said, "and you think badly of me. I want you to like me."

She started coming toward me and gazed at me seriously. Although the smile with which she'd looked at *Olympia* was glimmering in her eyes. She came very close and rubbed against me. She raised her head and there was no longer a smile in her eyes. There wasn't even a look. It's hard for me to define what was in her eyes. And then my desire grew to such hellish power that I found in it the strength to oppose it. However, I don't know whether I really found this strength in it, which is perhaps a little paradoxical. The fact is that I found the strength, although I didn't at all expect this.

I seized Helena by the arms and began shaking her. I didn't do so particularly brutally or violently. More like a doctor who wishes to bring back someone who's had a shock. Personally I very much dislike these allegedly decisive men who by means of violent words and gestures try to convince women of their masculine predominance. They're mostly mean hypocrites and egocentrics who like to sentimentalize over themselves.

I wasn't looking at Helena, but somewhere above her.

"Helena," I said, "come to your senses. Go away this minute and remember that we can't see one another any more. Something strange has happened, but we can't give way to it. I only want to tell you . . . I have to tell you . . . no, no, I won't tell you anything. What for? As it is you know everything, but go now. Go quickly."

I let her go. She lowered her head and began gathering the hair from her forehead.

"You're stupid," she said, "you're stupid. But never mind."

She turned, snatched the parasol and ran out so quickly that I hardly knew when it happened.

Then I threw myself on the bed and buried my head in the pillow.

I thought to myself, "Why the devil do I do everything in this way? To whom and in the name of what do I devote the charms which everyone chases after and which the majority regard as the proper aim of life?"

I do it because I have to. I do it because I started.

It was already ten after seven. I was still lying unthinkingly in
the bathtub. Maybe not so unthinkingly after all. But I was lying
there and I might be late. To all Agnieszka's faults was added her
terrible punctuality. Of course I don't regard punctuality in general as a vice. I was very punctual myself and couldn't bear unpunctual people. However, it was rather strange that with Agnieszka at times even a virtue looked like a fault. Surely because
she carried it about with particular ostentation and used it to
bother people. Probably my watch was a little fast. Not too much,
but a few minutes. It was a waterproof watch. I got it from the
club when I "did in" the English so nicely. It was really thanks to
me that we won that match. In my opinion that was too little
stressed. But it doesn't matter to me.

Of course, it's stupid to take a bath with a watch on, even a
waterproof one. But the fact that water can't get into it amused
me. It really can't. Well, and after all I knew what time it was
even while bathing. In this case I knew it only for the purpose of
knowing I was late. However, it was necessary to limit this catas-
trophe as far as possible. I suddenly leaped from the bathtub, the
water splashed beautifully and resounded on the tiled floor. I
started to dry myself rapidly. Combing my hair was the work of
three seconds, dressing and putting my shoes on, twenty-seven. I
checked the time on my watch, which was not only waterproof,
antimagnetic, and shockproof, but also had a stop device. By the
way, the club was spending heavily at that time. Generally, they
weren't too generous and magnanimous. I suspected that the English were merely a pretext. At that time, elections were going to be
held and people in the old administration were very anxious for
votes. The fact is that in actuality I voted for the old administration and persuaded others to do so, though at first I hadn't intended to. But I did it really in the entire conviction of the right-
ness of their case, and the suspicion that this might have some
connection with the watch came into my head much later.

When I ran out of the house, four minutes and six seconds were
left to me before the appointed meeting. Taking into consideration the few minutes my watch was fast, I didn't need to be late. If
I ran, then of course I'd not only make it in time, but would have

time to spare. However, it wasn't seemly for me to run through Cracow in a dark suit. Fortunately I caught a taxi immediately in front of the house and, with a feeling of triumph, as though I'd won a race at the Olympics, I drove up to the "Dawn" cinema, in other words the Cracow Philharmonic, a minute and three seconds ahead of time.

Agnieszka wasn't there yet. Movement, talk, an atmosphere of excitement and peculiar uneasiness prevailed in front of the Philharmonic. I liked this atmosphere. It reminded me of the atmosphere prior to a boxing match. Today the stake was very high. The best pianist in the world, ho ho. I wondered what sort of man he was. What he thinks when he plays. Automobiles were driving up, disgorging people and driving away quickly. The horizon over the houses in the depths of Zwierzyniecka Street was growing pink. I like these pinkening horizons that frequently glow over houses at dusk or at dawn. At dawn it was more beautiful. The glow, which acted optimistically and encouraged a person to go beyond these houses on the horizon. It seemed that it would be possible to find something extremely satisfying there, something one looks for all one's life although one doesn't know too well what it is. No great intelligence is required to realize quickly that beyond the houses on the horizon there will be other houses on the horizon with an aquamarine or pink glow and the promise of that which isn't known but which is sought for all through life. Of course they don't necessarily have to be houses; fields and woods will do. But this doesn't alter the essence of the thing.

Every moment someone or other greeted me. People I knew well and those who, it seemed to me, I'd never seen in my life. It was already twenty-five after seven, and Agnieszka still hadn't come. With the dignity of a priest entering a sanctuary of art the fat, bald character who had cried at the masked ball in the Academy of Fine Arts as he played gypsy romances and tried to recite the *Ode to Youth* at the ball in our club stalked up. He bowed to me solemnly. I didn't recognize him, but he knew me, and that sufficed him. By the way, this man was surely attaining a full life in a way. Artur Wdowinski came up with the President. They were quarreling. Properly speaking they weren't quarreling, only Artur was justifying himself. She was walking along with a motionless face and not paying attention to him. This was what their quarrels looked like. The funniest thing was that Artur really married the President, something nobody expected. She kept a firm hold of him; he looked satisfied. I liked her for hardly ever saying anything. Nothing that would be unnecessary.

"Hi," called Artur, "how are you, you pride of the Polish stadiums?"

He knew it irritated me when he called me this, and he did it on purpose. Sometimes he liked to tease people, just as a child or a girl does. As a man of the theater he had a girlish perversity in him.

"Good evening," said the President.

"Good evening, Ela," I said, "how can you stand it with that ropewalker?"

The President shrugged and Artur pulled her by the hand.

"Let's go," he said, "we're late. Will you drop by after the concert?"

As a rule after interesting concerts people went to Artur's, where there were always drinks of some sort. Supposedly to talk over the concert. Basically, to tipple; if the concert were talked over, it wasn't so much from the musical point of view as the social. Agnieszka still wasn't there. I was looking round and didn't notice the Ksiezaks coming up from the side. I'd have tried to hide from them, if I'd caught sight of them earlier.

"Hello," said Ksiezak, as if nothing had happened. "Well, what? Going in?"

"Yes, but Agnieszka is late."

Helena said nothing, merely smiled mysteriously. She always smiled stupidly in that way when the three of us were together. It irritated me so much that not only did she cease to please me, but I really started to dislike her. Even though I knew she only did it out of embarrassment. However, she looked so beautiful that even in this irritating moment I couldn't stop liking her. If, at the time when she came to me with Ksiezak's infernal memo she reminded me of something between a Saxon porcelain figurine and Brigitte Bardot, then today I'd have compared her rather to something midway between Marilyn Monroe in the role of a street girl and the Duchess of Kent during the coronation of her sister. I forgot the existence of Ksiezak for a moment and glanced into Helena's eyes. She responded with a look in which it seemed to me that I observed something like an offer that at any moment she was ready to become my slave and in general I could do what I wanted with her.

"Well, where are you hiding?" I heard behind me Agnieszka's irritable voice. "I've been looking for you for fifteen minutes."

She was slightly out of breath. I wondered for a moment what to reply, and determined not to reply at all. It was already very late. Apart from that I was grateful to Agnieszka for appearing at this moment.

"Let's go," I said.

In the auditorium the musicians were tuning up; this is something which I personally quite like. It seemed factual and concrete. People were excited and were trying to conciliate social freedom with the solemn atmosphere. Many wore expressions as though it were they who were to appear today, or at least as though the whole thing was to their credit. The Ksiezaks sat a few rows in front of us. He made some sort of face at me, the significance of which I didn't know, and she pretended not to notice me. With her profile turned away, she seemed to be reading the program but time and again, peeped furtively in our direction. Michal Podgorski almost rushed into the auditorium. He always arrives at the last moment. Not to be unpunctual, but because he's so busy. He looked around. He was certainly looking for us, but at this moment the lights went out, applause resounded and the conductor appeared on the platform. He was a balding, fair-haired man in spectacles, around forty. His face seemed familiar to me.

"I know that guy from somewhere," I said to Agnieszka.

"Sit quiet," said Agnieszka in a stifled voice. "At least don't compromise yourself."

"Why 'at least'? What do you have in mind?"

She gazed at me with a look in which there was nothing but pure hatred. I saw that she was simply losing control over herself. She made a movement as though she wanted to kick me in the ankle. She stopped herself at the last moment. I noticed she had new shoes. Pretty, with very pointed tips.

"What's this?" I asked, "did you buy new shoes today?"

She sighed helplessly and shifted away from me as far as she could.

"If you say another word, I'll move," she said.

"All the seats are taken. You'll have to sit on someone's knees."

Agnieszka turned her head away. Probably she started to cry. I felt badly. It must be awful to love someone whom one doesn't like so much. I ought to be better to her. After all, her rage only came from the conviction that something between us wasn't quite in order. I recalled where I knew that guy from. I had played poker with him at Artur's birthday party. He played very poorly and lost a lot. Let's see how it will go for him here. He raised his hands and put on an expression as though he were slightly angry with the players. They drew themselves up, and it's certainly a stupid comparison but it was altogether reminiscent of the start of a hundred-yard race.

The work was depressing and boring. Not even contemporary. For I liked contemporary music, despite everything. I didn't understand anything and that too bored me, but at the same time it was to a certain extent fascinating. I put out one hand to take the program from Agnieszka, and involuntarily placed my palm on hers. It was too late to withdraw or extricate myself. So I confirmed the gesture and lightly pressed her fingers. She kept hold of my hand, turned her face toward me and smiled. I was glad that a relaxation of tension had taken place between us so accidentally. Although, on the other hand, it was unbearable. Wouldn't it be better to go away some place with Agnieszka? Maybe to move to Warsaw for good? I waited a moment, then took the program from her. The music was boring, but I liked the conductor's movements very much. It was undoubtedly an aesthetic spectacle. I glanced at the program. What they were playing was called *Episode at a Masked Ball*. I immediately started listening differently. In the work there was a mood and tension which I hadn't noticed, or rather hadn't caught at first. In addition, Karlowicz was a mountaineer and had tumbled into a ravine, or maybe an avalanche had carried him off. Be that as it may, it counted. *Episode at a Masked Ball*. There were moments when it seemed to me that I'd completely forgotten about Jowita. So it may have seemed, but it wasn't so and never could be. If any value existed in my life, which might be called permanent, that value was Jowita.

For some time Agnieszka and I never spoke on the subject of Jowita. It seemed unnecessary to me, since I regarded it as certain that she was Jowita. One day Agnieszka asked me:

"Have you stopped being interested in Jowita now?"

It wasn't one day, but one night. She woke me up to ask me. I wanted to sleep and said:

"But not at all, darling. I'm very interested in her. Do I have to convince you of that?"

I wanted to embrace her, but she repelled me angrily.

"In the first place, you're trivial, and in the second you're an ass. All in all, you're a trivial stubborn ass and I don't like that. I'm really not Jowita, but she genuinely exists."

She said this with such conviction that I felt it mattered a great deal to her that I believed in it, so I was surprised and woke up.

"Very well," I said, "so be it. But I don't understand why you keep coming back to an incident I've already entirely forgotten. What are you concerned about?"

"I'm concerned precisely about the fact that you've so completely forgotten about this incident. She didn't forget you."

"Incident?"

"Jowita."

"Listen, darling, if Jowita really exists then it's you, so it seems, who's trying to push me into her arms. I swear to you there are a hundred and fifty better ways to free oneself of a man one doesn't love. But the best way is to tell him that directly, after which leave and cross to the other side of the street if one meets him."

At first Agnieszka didn't reply. She was silent a long time and I started to be afraid lest she approve of my advice as correct and lest she were getting ready to inform me of this.

She placed her hands under her head and, gazing at the ceiling, said:

"It really isn't me. It's you who always introduce an ambiguous atmosphere when we start talking about Jowita. For example, now. I asked you whether you'd stopped entirely being interested in Jowita, because a few days ago I had a letter from her, in which she literally asks: 'Does that man from the masked ball still remember me?' "

"And you wake me up in the night to tell me that?"

"Oh, I'm sorry. Oh, I'm very sorry that I interrupted your bourgeois slumber. I promise you won't be exposed to anything of the sort again."

She jumped out of bed. To get dressed and leave, for sure. I managed to grab her by the leg and pull her back. Agnieszka had moral domination over me. But sometimes, when I got mad, she became meek. Generally speaking I didn't take refuge in my physical superiority. I regarded that as unseemly in relations with women. Apart from that I was convinced it led nowhere. Maybe I was wrong. For sometimes when I got mad, Agnieszka would become strangely mild, and it even seemed to me that she liked it. So I pulled her back into bed by her leg, seized her hand forcefully so that it must surely have hurt her, since she squealed, and then I leaned over her.

"And now," I said, "you're going to tell me without any joshing or fooling everything about Jowita from start to finish. If you don't, I'll give you such a whipping that you won't be able to sit down for several days and you'll have to paint standing up."

"One usually paints standing up," said Agnieszka in a

sweet voice. "In this respect it won't mean anything."

I reflected that I should be so decisive more often. Maybe always. Who knows whether then my relations with Agnieszka might not work out differently. But when a person takes something into his head on the subject of his behavior, then nothing helps. Not even experience drawn from practice. No one knows whether a higher power decides this or the devil knows what, but the fact is that people in general behave quite differently from the way they intend to behave. In some cases even differently from the way it seems to them they're behaving.

In any case, Agnieszka suddenly became another person. She smiled sweetly and lazily, rubbed her head a few times against my cheek and began talking about Jowita. I let her be, leaned my head against her shoulder and listened.

Jowita's parents had emigrated to Australia before the war and she was born there. Polish traditions were maintained in the house, she went to a Polish school, considered herself Polish, and felt more strongly attached to Poland than to the country in which she was born and bred. Agnieszka didn't know where the strange name Jowita came from. Jowita had told her, but Agnieszka didn't remember very well. In any case, it is a very Slavic name. Apparently Jowita's great-grandmother bore it, an insurgent of the year 1863, sort of an Emilia Plater on a smaller scale. Agnieszka isn't sure whether she didn't mix up the grandmother with the name. When they met Jowita, they had so much to say that they often talked at once and then one didn't recall what the other had said. In any case, what does it matter? Her name was Jowita, and that was that. So Jowita, on graduating from high school, had decided to come to Poland to do graduate work. She came immediately after graduating and registered at the School of Journalism, but her hobby was photography. She underwent training in Warsaw with the best photographers and apparently had great talent in this line. Agnieszka had gotten to know her the previous year at Kalatowki during the jamboree and they at once became friends. She really was an exceptional girl. Full of life, intelligence, wit, and in general all the virtues. Agnieszka couldn't come to terms with the idea that Jowita had already left, that maybe she would never see her again. Well, but it wasn't this that mattered, but rather the unusual meeting at the masked ball. So Jowita had come to Cracow then to visit Agnieszka, since they'd agreed to go to this masked ball together. This was to have been the last big farewell to Poland, for immediately afterwards Jowita was returning to Australia for good. Unfortunately it didn't work out. The day before, Agnieszka came down with a bad case of flu. Jowita didn't want to go without her but the fellows with whom they'd made dates came, and she let herself be persuaded. She didn't dress up in any costume, because that wasn't her style. She had quite a good time. She's the kind that always has a good time and everybody who's with her must have a good time too. Toward morning, she met Mika in the cloakroom, who was taking off her Eastern costume to put on a dress and go home. She asked her to let her try it on. Something had suddenly entered her head. She was curious how she'd look in it and how she'd feel. Well, and then she met me. As Agnieszka declares, she immediately felt an enormous liking for me. She really wanted to leave with me. She hurried away to change, but when she came out in front of the Academy, where we'd arranged to meet, she had a huge disappointment in store.

"She came up to you," said Agnieszka, "but you didn't recognize her. She came up to you with a smile and said: 'What now?' and you glanced at her angrily and replied: 'Let me be, for goodness sake. Go accost somebody else.' Then she walked away, came home and told me all of it, with details. It's a sad story."

I lay beside Agnieszka and was silent.

"It's impossible," I said, after a moment.

"What's impossible? Why? Don't the facts agree?"

"Yes. But it's impossible that I'd reply so rudely to any woman."

"Ah, it only seems so to you. You know how to be very vulgar at times."

"Me vulgar?"

"You don't see it, but it's so. People even comment on it."

Referring to the opinion of unspecified people is the most treacherous argument of women in disputes with us. It's hard to disprove them. A man becomes pushed into the defensive and after a while begins to seem guilty to himself. The squabble about my brutal forms of existence proceeded a long time, although this time not particularly violently. I was pleased by this. I could conceal the impression which Agnieszka's tale had made on me. It all seemed to be really true. But how is it possible that I didn't recognize Jowita? My own Jowita? I didn't know her face, of course. But her eyes? And her figure altogether? All of her, who in the course of fifteen minutes or so had seemed to me the closest being on the earth?

"Forget all this, Agnieszka," I said. "If Jowita feels insulted, I can apologize to her at any time."

"And you still dare to claim that you're not a boor? You're a terrible boor. To think that poor Jowita left believing she'd met the most delicate, subtle, and unusual person in the world."

"Even though I spoke to her so coarsely?"

"Even though. She believed it was because you were waiting for her and that all women other than herself irritated you."

"And she was right," I exclaimed triumphantly, "but why didn't she say it was she?"

"You know, that was the last straw, for a girl you've picked up, proposed some ambiguous breakfast to, and in general almost want to marry, for this girl suddenly to present herself."

"But it was late at night, or even early morning, and I was soused. Well, I may have made a mistake."

"You may, you may," Agnieszka muttered, "but it really isn't essential for you to justify yourself to me so violently that you didn't seduce another girl."

Rage seized me, but I said calmly:

"You monkey, you. I'm wondering what I'm to do with you, and I've no idea."

Agnieszka said nothing. I didn't say anything either and then we fell asleep, a little mad at each other, but in the morning we made up and I remained with only a vague recollection of this nocturnal conversation. Despite everything I continued to believe that Jowita was Agnieszka although, to tell the truth, I began to doubt it somewhat.

Agnieszka was renting a room with distant relatives in Wislana Street. There weren't any regulations governing the room and her relatives, a middle-aged married couple, were rarely at home. Despite this I didn't much like going there to see her. But not long after this conversation about Jowita, Agnieszka caught a cold and stayed in bed, so I had to go there. She always caught cold easily, which irritated me. Despite this I was very good to her, which actually touched me more than it did her. I came every morning, brought her flowers and various trifles, I cleaned the room and arranged meals. I also brought her letters from the mailbox downstairs. One morning I drew out a long blue envelope with a stamp bearing a kangaroo. The letter was from Australia. I glanced at the sender's address. It read: Jowita Gawryluk, 758 Mahagony Street, Sydney W. I held this letter in my hand for a long time, overcome by an emotion impossible to define. By a sort of instinct I wanted to put it away in my pocket and not hand it to Agnieszka but of course immediately rejected this thought. When I handed it to Agnieszka, she said:

"It's from Jowita. How pleased I am. She hasn't written in a long time."

She tore open the envelope, removed the letter and began reading. Reading, she smiled, uttered murmurs and little cries and did a number of similar things capable of leading into a fever anyone interested in the contents of a letter not addressed to him and who doesn't want to show it.

"My dearest, sweetest Jowita," said Agnieszka, when she'd finished reading, and she kissed the letter. "She longs for us here terribly. I'm very sorry but this time she doesn't mention you."

I thought she'd give me the letter to read, but she placed it back in the envelope and put it away under her pillow as though afraid I'd want to steal it.

"She had great success at a photographic exhibition in Melbourne," Agnieszka finally said, "she won a money prize and life is working out wonderfully well for her. Nevertheless, she keeps thinking of coming back to us."

I controlled myself and am sure Agnieszka didn't notice my emotion. I left promptly.

The orchestra stopped playing. Quite suddenly. So it seemed to me in any case. The silence brought me back to reality, and immediately afterwards applause confirmed me in it.

"Were you asleep or what?" said Agnieszka. "You look as if you were. Really, you don't have to come to concerts if they bore you."

"For goodness sake!" I replied. "I immersed myself entirely in the music. The conductor was magnificent."

"He led them a little too slowly," said Agnieszka in a careless tone.

I hated it when she acted so knowingly and uttered professional opinions about things she wasn't an expert on.

There was movement on the platform, which I liked. They pushed chairs back and brought forward the piano. I liked these preparations most of all. Helena turned and was gazing at me. I didn't look in that direction, but could feel that insistent gaze upon me. It irritated me a little, and moved me a little. An atmosphere of solemn excitement prevailed in the auditorium. It was summoned up by the nearness of the appearance of the greatest pianist in the world. Who, I keep asking, had measured him? In what direct encounters did he display his superiority to all the others? Agnieszka twisted in her seat and had flushed cheeks.

"There he is," she said suddenly.

There was a great commotion, more or less like that on a crowded railroad station platform when an international express is arriving. All this time I could feel Helena's furtive gaze. Loud applause resounded, and even shouts. People stood up. He walked on to the platform. Behind him the conductor-poker player already known to me, deliberately showing that he was unimportant here and simply didn't count, as he tried all the more desperately to attract attention. The pianist stopped in the center of the platform and started bowing. He was a handsome, grizzled man around fifty. Of medium height, obviously a bungler. He bowed in the fashion of a maestro; also he raised his hands to greet the audience. The ovation continued and reached a point where both the object of the applause and those applauding would have wanted it to stop, but somehow it wasn't possible to halt it, like a runaway motor car in which the brakes have failed. Here the conductor demonstrated unheard-of experience and presence of mind. He himself stopped clapping in a firm and decided manner and, turning to the orchestra, he raised his baton slightly. The orchestra players sat down and then the audience sat down too and of course it was necessary for the pianist to sit down at the piano. Silence fell. He struck a note and he and the conductor exchanged signals. Helena wasn't looking at me any more, but now I gazed at her and readily saw by her shoulders that she was thinking about me. In my opinion, shoulders are often more expressive than a face.

The artist straightened himself on the stool. I very much like all the things that happen at concerts before the music starts. Suddenly: crash! The orchestra started with a frightful din.

Even he jumped, as though it had startled him. But assuredly he did it on purpose, in order to demonstrate what a great impression the music made on him. Not a bad gesture. Even I was somehow drawn into it. I took the program from Agnieszka, who didn't notice. Her cheeks were flushed. She was only half conscious. If anything of the sort could still enter into the game, I'd probably be jealous of this champion. The work he was playing or which, properly speaking, he was about to start playing, for meanwhile the orchestra was showing off alone, was called the Piano Concerto in D minor, the composer, Johannes Brahms. I liked the name. I would like to be called Brahms. Although I'd prefer some other first name. For instance Howard or Allan. No. Rather not Allan. Properly speaking not Howard much, either. The champ was sitting somehow modestly on his stool. He seemed mournful and sad to me. Sometimes he raised his head slightly and listened to the orchestra attentively. Exactly as though he were making up his mind what and how to play when his turn came. What was this comedy of his own decision and his own will for? All that would happen was what Mr. Allan Howard Brahms had long since decided already. It isn't the same as a race of fifteen hundred or five thousand meters, where there's no score and the action of the drama has to be created by the help of superhuman willpower, in full view of a gathering of people, and really it isn't known right up to the tape what the outcome will be. I very much wanted to do some running over longer distances. I very much wanted to take part in the Memorial. But if I did, if I succeeded in gaining a victory, I'd owe it all to Ksiezak. But I couldn't and didn't want to owe anything to Ksiezak. That donkey didn't understand why I sulked with him and he regarded me as a spoiled prima donna. Of course he didn't understand. How could he?

Something was starting to happen there on the platform. The orchestra slowed down, grew quiet. The conductor was making gestures as though his strength was already failing. He looked around for help. The champ suddenly straightened up: What? Don't you have the strength? Is the music which you started with such vigor dying and falling silent? I listened to your playing and didn't intend to interfere. But I see that without me you will all perish. So I will hasten to your aid.

Lightly, like a knight fanning a swooning lady with a flower, he began striking the keys, and the orchestra replied with a quiet groan. The virtuoso started playing louder and louder and with ever increasing firmness. The swooning orchestra ever more clearly was returning to consciousness. But when the piano recalled its triumphant start, it was already restored to its senses, strong, courageous, and heroic. With a step once more firm and decisive it was following after him who had raised it from collapse.

An interesting thing, by the way. Although I didn't understand music, I wasn't bored this time and what was taking place on the platform impressed me in some way. It aroused my imagination. The champ must really have been quite strong. He was able to fascinate me by his external action alone, though it wasn't easy to take me in by such tricks. A tense and heated atmosphere was growing in the auditorium. What this Chapayev of the piano was producing was really unusual and overwhelming. What must it have been for those who in addition understood music! And at this time he wasn't a bungler. Not at all. In the auditorium several hundred musical bunglers were sitting and I was a bungler among them, though an unmusical one. But now he wasn't a bun-

gler. Helena turned her head for an instant. She was seeking me
with her gaze. She smiled. By this smile and look she wanted to
inform me that, although subjected to the general emotion and
general tension, she hadn't stopped thinking about me. What was
it all for, Helena, ah Helena? What was it to me and to you?
Wouldn't it have been better if there at your place we'd committed the crime dictated to us by nature? Or, that later time at my
place. We'd have had it behind us and maybe would even have
erased the traces of the crime, which comes so easily to people in
the face of this sort of crime. Why did I resist so much that I even
rejected the appeal of nature, which mocks conventions invented
by people and takes her revenge when one goes counter to her dic-
tates.

Helena phoned me the very evening of the day she had brought
Ksiezak's memo and I had told her to leave.

"Marek," she said, "do you know you threw me out of your
house?"

"I know."

"Probably you did right."

"I'm glad you think so. No. I'm not glad."

"I'm not glad either, but I know you did right. Do you know
why I'm calling?"

"No."

"I don't know either. So we won't be seeing each other any
more?"

"We oughtn't to."

"Tell me why it's like this."

"Like what?"

"We've been acquainted for a few years and we never really
noticed one another, but now . . ."

"Better end this conversation."

"You're right. Goodbye."

She put down the receiver.

I don't know how it happened that we met a few days later. We
talked about not being able to meet. And now we kept on meeting
to talk about this. Nothing happened between us. We didn't even
kiss. And yet I had a more guilty conscience than if we'd committed what some call perfidy. The atmosphere in and around us was
kindling and swelling up. It seemed impossible that the volcano
wouldn't finally explode. If it exploded, however, I'd become a
villain and I didn't want to be a villain. I knew I was a zero. I
didn't represent any genuine value for the world of nature and

mankind. All I could offer them and myself was not to become a villain. Admittedly humanity would never learn of this generous gift, but what of it?

He was driving ahead, no doubt aiming for the end. He was really extraordinary. I was scared Agnieszka would faint. How embarrassing that would have been! It seemed to me that not only the audience but the orchestra too was in a state of unusually solemn excitement. Everyone had forgotten the conductor. Suddenly he pulled off a completely fantastic stunt. He put down his baton and stepped off the podium. As though he were completely unnecessary. He, with his masterly playing, will lead the orchestra. O maestro of maestros! I'm thinking in this case of the conductor. All the same he'd done this in order to draw a little attention to himself and to distinguish himself. The last chords were sounding, he sat a moment longer at the piano with bowed head and hands hanging down and for a moment an improbable silence prevailed. First to penetrate it was the conductor. He raised his hands, uttered a cry and went up to the piano. In this manner he indicated that he was no longer the conductor but an enthusiastic listener who couldn't control himself and had to render homage to the maestro. I was ready to bet he was striving for concerts in America. Still, the enthusiasm which later followed seemed to me sincere and genuine. I myself yielded to it although of course not to the same degree as others. After the conductor's gesture, the maestro rose and bowed, and for a moment he pressed the hands of the conductor who had come up to him. He held him by these hands. The conductor tried to break away, but the maestro wouldn't yield and forced him into bowing together with him. The former finally yielded with a conspiratorial smile directed at the audience. As though it were necessary to give way to the caprices of the maestro but it wasn't necessary to take these bows seriously. However, the conductor made a fool of himself quite unnecessarily. Apart from me surely no one was paying any attention to him. What happened in the auditorium is indescribable. People jumped from their seats overwhelmed by a kind of collective madness. Someone not far from me was sobbing loudly, the air shook with bravos and shouts, I heard something beside me fall to the ground and was scared to look. Agnieszka? No. She'd merely dropped her handbag. She didn't even notice. She was red in the face, trembling like most of the people around. Under other circumstances such a state of collective excitement leads to lynchings. He bowed and bowed. Again he was a bungler and didn't impress me at all. By the way, I never saw such madness or such an ovation on any sports field. It's sometimes happened that I've received enthusiastic cheers and once they even carried me out of a stadium on their shoulders. But I'd never even imagined anything like this. The conductor grew sad and lost the initiative. He stood to one side among the violinists and put on a mournful expression. It seemed to me that he was very tired of all this and already in general it was all the same to him. Maybe he had domestic troubles, and when the tension passed he recollected it? I felt sorry for him.

The maestro left the platform and came back many times, summoned by the applause. I wanted it to stop. I wanted this concert to stop and I wanted to go to Artur's. Although I really didn't know whether it would be all that amusing for me. The Ksiezaks would certainly come too. Ksiezak, Agnieszka, Helena, and I—together in a relatively small space—was a rather too powerful cast. I thought it would be better to go to bed. Yes, I'll take myself off to bed and that's it. The bravos finally stopped. People looked weary. Like the conductor previously. They had a slight hangover as one usually has after ostentatious displays of feeling. Agnieszka drew one hand across her brow.

"Shall we go to Artur's?" I asked.

She didn't reply. She was assuredly dazed by the emotion she'd experienced or which she had persuaded herself of, but I knew her well enough to observe there was uneasiness within her this day, which she was trying to conceal from me. It seemed to me that something was bothering her, that maybe she wanted to tell me something and kept holding back.

Did she guess that there was something between Helena and me? How could she possibly guess it? Women don't need special means in order to guess such things. Apart from this, there are surely enough women in Cracow who might have seen Helena and me and informed Agnieszka. I began feeling a little as I did once before a Sunday match when I tried to conceal from Szymaniak that I'd flunked a Polish composition.

We went out of the rows and walked in silence toward the exit. I could feel that something was about to happen. That something was gathering and must explode. In the vestibule I unfortunately ran straight into the Ksiezaks. He was idiotically excited. He began exchanging impressions with Agnieszka. It seemed to me however that Agnieszka was watching Helena and me sideways. She did it so discreetly that it was hard for me to say whether it really was so. But I felt that it was.

"Are you going to Artur's?" I asked, for the sake of saying something.

The stubborn silence of Helena and me seemed to me something like an admittance of guilt.

"Of course not," said Ksiezak, "after all I'm leaving for Warsaw immediately after the concert."

I'd forgotten that Ksiezak had written another memo. Michal Podgorski appeared, bowed to us from a distance but didn't come over.

I didn't understand why. Apparently he didn't like the Ksiezaks.

"But I'll be grateful to you," said Ksiezak, "if you two will take Helena along."

"I'm not going without you," said Helena.

"You're carrying things too far," said Ksiezak, "with this holding on to me like to mother's skirts. You can't take a single step without me."

"Well, for a half hour at most," said Helena.

"Will you both see her home afterwards?" asked Ksiezak.

"I can't go either," said Agnieszka, "my aunt from Poznan has come. It was difficult for me to get away for the concert."

This was the first time I'd heard of any aunt from Poznan.

I glanced at Agnieszka. She turned her head away. The conversation and all this together was unbearable.

"Listen," she said suddenly, "you must go backstage and bring me his autograph. I must have this autograph. Oh, on this program."

She handed me the program.

"Why can't you go yourself?"

"Obviously I can go myself," said Agnieszka in a voice in which hysteria lurked.

I understood I must go. More than that! I understood that I hadn't the right to come back without the autograph. To ask a man for his autograph was something simply awful. But in the end it was better than standing around as we did and exchanging phrases in which the power of an atomic explosion was slumbering. I walked away with relief.

The stage entrance was besieged. An attendant, with the look of a man incapable of compromises, was defending it. He was the father of Piotr Marchewka, a pole vaulter in our club. He recognized me and immediately let me in. Backstage the crush was no less than at the entrance. The lucky ones who'd succeeded in getting through were besieging the maestro with outstretched programs. I didn't see any opportunity of getting near him, but decided not to give up. Not only for fear of Agnieszka, but on account of myself. Since I'd made the decision to do it, I must carry it out to the end. All the more since I had a natural dislike of it. I joined in the circle closely surrounding the maestro, but the chances of getting through to him still seemed scanty. At one moment the maestro looked up and our eyes met. He frowned a moment, eyeing me, finally smiled, pushed back the people surrounding him, and approached me. Everyone was looking at me, and I most probably had an expression such as that time in school when it got out that it was I who had smeared the blackboard with ink, and the teacher was coming up to me playing with the cane he held in one hand. Of course he didn't dare hit me, and I didn't expect that in the least. But his gaze, the sudden silence and the gazes of my classmates summoned up an idiotic grin on my face. I suppose it was just like the smile with which I was now looking at the approaching champion from Los Angeles. Now what does he want?

"Surely I'm not mistaken that you're Marek Arens," he said, stretching out a hand. I seized it rather clumsily.

"Yes, I am," I answered quietly.

"You can't imagine what a pleasure it is for me that you're visiting me. A few weeks ago I was applauding you in the stadium at Rome. Sports is my hobby, sir, and I am primarily interested in Polish sports. I subscribe to the 'Sports Review' and know all the results by heart."

Just look, ladies and gentlemen! I knew he must be a bungler, but I never thought he'd be such a big one. He aroused in me mixed feelings of like and dislike. He took the program from my hands and without even asking if I wanted him to, wrote his autograph. I'd had enough mortification, for sure, but at least it was good that I wouldn't go back to Agnieszka with empty hands. It would cost me dearly.

"Thank you, sir," I said.

I turned and walked away quickly. I had the impression I ought to have said something more, to have stayed longer and to have talked. But I couldn't. My one desire was to disappear as fast as I could.

In the passage, which was already deserted after the bell, I sighed with relief. I glanced at the program. Well, the joker had let me down nicely.

On the program was written: "To Marek Arens with admiration and liking."

I preferred not even to think what the results of this would be if I showed Agnieszka the program with such an autograph. I looked discreetly around, tore up the program and threw it into a wastebasket.

I don't understand how it came to this! I can't even remember the moment in which it happened.

Light was dazzling me and my head ached. I thought of everything that had happened and simply couldn't grasp it.

And this lamp was irritating me terribly. I wanted to sleep.

"For God's sake, turn off the lamp," I said.

"Don't call upon the name of the Lord in vain. And if the lamp is dazzling you, turn over."

"Is this really the proper time for reading books?"

"A citizen of Peoples' Poland should take advantage of every moment for self-education. You too can read a little, if you want. Or I'll read aloud to you. Do you want me to?"

"No, no. Only I implore you."

"Well then, no. After all you can sleep. Put your head on my hip. Here. Or here. Come on. Don't be scared. How come you're so bashful? I didn't think it of you. I imagined you were different. And what did you imagine about me?"

"I didn't imagine anything. I want to sleep and my head aches."

"You're too young to do such things. Go to sleep. Put your head here. Here. Yes, now you'll be all right. I'll stroke your hair and you'll fall asleep right away."

"You don't have to stroke my hair."

"I don't have to, but I want to. It gives me pleasure. When I was young, I had a big doll with marvelous hair. In the evening I put her next to me in bed and fell asleep stroking her hair. You're a little like that doll. Otherwise I'd never have allowed you to lie in bed with me."

"Wouldn't you?"

"Certainly not. Or how should I know? Well, go to sleep now."

I cuddled up to her warm, vigorous body and for a while it was good. It seemed to me I was that doll with marvelous hair. It wouldn't be bad to be a doll, which has absolutely nothing inside except perhaps sawdust, to lie motionless like this without feeling. One can tell oneself for consolation that this is only a dream, which sooner or later will assuredly be fulfilled. The thought of the doll had a calming effect on me. The whole world and all its problems had been set in the inconclusive dimensions of childhood. I'd almost fallen asleep when the sudden awareness of what had happened pierced my heart with a sharp pain.

Where's Agnieszka now? What's she doing? What's she thinking?

I will account to fate for my acts. If there's no court to mete out punishment and penitence for being false to honor and faith, not to mention a broken vow taken over the grave of one's mother, then I myself will create such a tribunal.

After the concert, Artur forced everyone to go to his place. I tried to slip away but didn't succeed. To make matters worse, we bumped into the Ksiezaks again. Was it only by chance?

"I implore you both," said Ksiezak, "take Helena with you. I have to rush to the station and she always gets upset when I leave and she's alone."

"I don't get upset in the least," said Helena, with a fury so out of proportion to the subject that it must have surprised everyone. Everyone except Ksiezak.

"You see," he said, "she's upset already. She can't remain alone, because she hasn't anyone to talk to. More than anything else in the world she likes talking. If there's nobody to talk to, then . . . then . . ."

He didn't know what to say.

"Then she's silent," Agnieszka finished. She gazed at Helena with a slight smile. I didn't like that smile. Helena shrugged, as though she'd reached the conclusion that it wasn't worth prolonging this dialogue. Ksiezak smiled foolishly. He sensed that something wasn't in order, but he didn't know what.

"Then she's silent," he confirmed, "just so."

"Let Marek and Helena go to Artur's together in that case," said Agnieszka, "for I still have to torture myself with this unhappy aunt."

"I never before saw you making such a fuss over relatives. Are you counting on an inheritance from this aunt?"

I said this aggressively, not knowing why, and instantly regretted it. But Agnieszka accepted the aggression calmly.

"You're stupid," she said, "and if you can't fix such a stupid matter as an autograph, you'd better not try to be malicious. I'll try to get rid of my aunt as quickly as possible. And then I'll come to Artur's. I think you two will manage somehow without me."

By this last phrase she almost openly informed us that she knew everything.

"My dear children," said Ksiezak, "I'm late. Let's go."

He stopped a passing taxi.

"Be off with you," said Agnieszka, "I'm going in the other direction."

Before I could say anything to her, she turned and walked away. I called after her "Agnieszka!" but she didn't hear or pretended not to.

"Marek," said Ksiezak in the taxi, "we've talked so much nonsense today and in general in the past few days. But now we must exchange a few words without hysteria. We must talk like men."

"What do you want of him?" cried Helena, who was sitting next to the driver. "What are you attacking him for? He's got nothing to say to you."

"Really, Helena," said Ksiezak, "you're making too much of a fool of yourself today. You must be sick. What are you really concerned about? Anyway, never mind what you're concerned about, because that can't concern Marek. I implore you, however, that you be good enough to let us exchange a few words. Listen, Marek. You know very well I'm going to Warsaw in connection with your case too. And you know very well that it's necessary finally . . ."

"Edward," I said, "I've been behaving and am behaving stupidly toward you. Please don't get mad. But please also don't let's talk any more about this matter. I won't be starting in the Memorial."

"Marek, one more word . . ."

"I won't be starting in the Memorial, and in addition to that, as soon as I can discharge various club obligations, I'll withdraw from sports."

"Why do you want to abandon sports? For heaven's sake! After all, it's the basis of your life."

"That's exactly why. And because I don't want to be beholden to anyone."

"But whom are you beholden to?"

"Let's not talk any more about all this."

Ksiezak was silent, depressed. I was sorry, but I couldn't do anything about it. Helena was angrily muttering something under her breath.

We drove onto Jan Street to the front of the house where Artur lived. Helena and I got out, while Ksiezak, who was going on, to the railroad station, suddenly grew cheerful, seized by an instinct of wholesome optimism.

"But I know," he said, changing his seat to the place by the driver, "that you'll be starting in the Memorial. I already know your changing moods. Anything at all will jar on you and discourage you. You're a mimosa. The fastest mimosa in the world. But you won't abandon sports and you'll start in the Memorial. Helena! Wait a moment, Helena, do you want to bet that Marek will start in the Memorial?"

"Oh for goodness sake, leave me alone," cried Helena, and holding her head in both hands she ran into the gateway.

The taxi drove away with the suddenly absurdly cheerful Ksiezak. I went toward the gateway, prepared for another depressing scene. This time with Helena, who was so obviously off balance. But really one never knows with women. When I went in, Helena, concealed behind the gateway, jumped out with a wanton cry, hoping to startle me as it were. She fell upon me and leaned against my chest, holding me by my lapels. Her amused eyes glowed in the dark.

"Alone at last," she said, and laughed. "Those spouses of ours are monstrous bores."

"Helena, did you notice that Agnieszka has guessed everything? I'm sure she's plotting something."

"You're imagining things, darling. And apart from that, what has she to plot? I don't feel like talking or thinking about all this today. I'm glad we're together and I want to amuse myself, have a drink and dance. With you. I terribly want to dance with you."

"But I tell you Agnieszka is plotting something. I know her."

"Well, let her get on with her plotting, and we'll go and have a good time."

She took me by the arm and we walked down a long, dark hallway toward the wooden stairs. At the foot of the stairs, Helena stopped. She cuddled up to me. Very lightly, but we'd never yet been so close to one another. I started to tremble and tried to control myself. I never wanted anyone or anything in my life as much as I wanted Helena.

"But what's it all about, really?" asked Helena, challengingly. "What's it all about? What right does Agnieszka have to plot anything, even if she does suspect something? Who in general can lay any blame on us? Aren't two people of the opposite sex allowed to meet in this accursed Cracow if they like one another? We've done nothing bad, and nobody could blame your behavior toward me. Apart from the fact that you grabbed me by the collar and threw me out of your house."

"I didn't take you by the collar. What are you saying? And anyway, I didn't throw you out of my house. You know very well that's not true. Just as you know that everything else you said a moment ago is untrue. Both true and untrue at the same time."

I was standing with my shoulder against the wall by the stairs, or strictly speaking against a sort of pillar or rather projection of the wall. I suddenly felt I was saying something which didn't concern me, which was at this moment entirely immaterial, because the one material thing was the closeness of Helena. I made a movement undefined in purpose, though objectively it must have looked like a defined one, for Helena drew back and hid behind the projection of the wall. After a moment she stuck her head out and gazed at me in the darkness.

"No, no," she began saying rapidly, as though scared she wouldn't be in time for something, that something would escape her, "no, no! I implore you. I don't want to. I beg you! I don't want to deceive Edward. I have never yet deceived him and I don't want to. I beg you, be off. Leave me here alone and go away as fast as you can, because after all you know as well as I, that . . . Well, go, go."

She stopped, but after a moment—this happened completely of its own accord, and neither she nor I can be blamed for it, of course in that given moment, not generally—after a moment we pressed our mouths together strongly and with the tension of a loaded atom which all the same was waiting for it like a devil imprisoned in a bottle some dozen or some hundred, or perhaps some millions or even billions of years. I don't really know how long, and don't believe those who say they know.

Then I heard a rustle behind me. Someone had come through the gateway and stopped on its threshold. I crouched down and wanted to hide behind the projection of the wall, but before I had time to do so, a flashlight illuminated me. It lit up for a moment, and instantly went out. Helena, half-conscious, was swooning in my arms with her head leaning back, lips parted and eyes closed, and didn't know what was going on around. I looked toward the gateway. In the gateway Agnieszka was standing. She was standing with feet slightly apart, holding the extinguished flashlight in her hand. I'd given her this flashlight for her birthday. It was a very fine flashlight made by Siemens, small, flat, with a rechargeable battery, it cost four hundred and fifty zloty in the commission store.

Agnieszka said, "Marek." She said it so quietly that I wondered whether I was imagining it. She stood motionless a while yet then turned around and disappeared behind the gateway.

Helena suddenly came to and straightened up.

"What happened?" she asked, rubbing her forehead with one hand, like someone aroused from deep sleep. "Who shone a flashlight here?"

"Nothing happened. Only Agnieszka came into the gateway and illuminated us with a flashlight."

"That's impossible."

"Why? It's entirely possible, because that's precisely what happened."

Helena said nothing. She bowed her head and stroked her hair with the indifference of a monkey amusing itself with a mirror. She swayed slightly on both feet, backward and forward. Finally she turned around and started going up the stairs.

I went after her at a certain distance and didn't think about anything. Helena reached Artur's door, rang, and then said, turning back to me:

"You're an impossible idiot. Quite impossible."

The door opened before I reached the landing. Helena went in. I turned back and ran down the stairs.

It really was very good. Leaning against that hip or, for the sake of accuracy, somewhere near the hip, half asleep and muffled by the yellow light of the lamp, I felt as though in some safe asylum.

"Did you fall asleep?" I asked.

"No. But don't get upset. I'll turn out the lamp right away."

"You don't have to turn it off."

"Oh, so kindly all of a sudden. A moment ago he was making a scene about the light, but now he's so kindly."

"You know what? It's good to be with you. I must state at three in the morning, that it's good to be with you."

"Big deal. It's always good for me to be with you."

"You know what, maybe I'll marry you."

"What, did you take a bath in the Vistula near the Wawel castle on a rainy day?"

"Where do you get such sayings from?"

"Where from? I make them up myself. And what of it? Do you think I'm too much of an idiot to make up such a thing by myself? In general, you consider me an idiot, admit it."

"Of course I do, darling. But for all that I'll marry you. I'll call your mother right away and ask for your hand in marriage."

I picked up the telephone and pretended I wanted to dial a number.

"Have you gone crazy? To call my mother at this hour? You can call tomorrow. Well, stop it! Stop it, will you? You can call tomorrow and ask for my hand in marriage. In any case, she won't agree. She says she'd sooner drop dead than see me married to an athlete. Please, stop it."

We started struggling. Dorota giggled and I started laughing. The telephone fell on the floor, and Dorota said:

"Now stop it. That's enough. What's gotten into you suddenly? It happened, it's over. I really implore you to leave me alone. I don't feel like it any more."

I picked up the telephone, calmly replaced it and put my hands under my head.

"So you say your mother won't let you marry me?"

"Certainly not."

"But do you obey her in everything?"

"Did you put your head into a bonfire in the Sahara? I don't listen to Mummy at all."

"Well, so what?"

"Well, nothing."

"Tell me, Dorota. Do you love me?"

Dorota frowned.

"Well, of course I don't love you. That means not in the way you're asking now. Because what you're concerned with is whether it's like the movies. Eh? Well, I don't love you like that. But if for instance you died, I'd surely not eat anything for three days. So what?"

"So nothing."

"In that case, open the vent and up! And let me read in peace. I'll finish it right away and there'll be peace. Give me an apple. No, don't. I'll get one myself; I'd feel sorry for you if you got up."

"Why?"

"How should I know? Somehow you're so pitiable. Afflicted, afflicted . . . well, how does one say it, I don't remember any more. The guys in the club talk to each other so. Some sort of brother or something. Remind me how it's said. I'll give you an apple too. Want one? But first remind me how it's said."

"It's not said at all. In any case, young girls don't say it. I don't want an apple."

Dorota got out of bed and went to the table. She was completely naked, but didn't display the slightest embarrassment. She was behaving with the grace and restraint of a young girl who has gone out for a Sunday morning walk in a newly made dress with her grandmother. There was nothing immodest in her nakedness, only the simplicity of original man, who didn't yet feel the need of hiding his body from the malicious caprices of nature. She came back to bed biting a large red apple. She might have been reminiscent of Eve, but she wasn't. In her there was nothing which might have been associated with sin. In the meaning of the catechism, of course. She lay down and took the book. It was *Peter Pan*.

"I'll finish it right away and tell you about it," she said, "meanwhile sleep. Properly speaking I ought to go home already. O Jesus, what will mother think? But let her think anything she wants. When she comes back from that actor of hers, I don't think anything. No? Well, what? No? Why don't you answer?"

"You were going to read and I was going to sleep."

"Oh, yes, you're right. Well, so don't say anything more."

How did this happen? How could this have happened?

I ran down the stairs and out into the street. As usual at this hour St. Jan Street was empty except for a couple of drunks who were loudly arguing somewhere near the Francuski Hotel. I didn't know whether Agnieszka had gone in that direction or toward the Market Place. In any case, what significance could it have? I didn't intend to pursue her. What could I say to her? No, it wasn't because of this that I'd run out. I didn't intend to run after Agnieszka. I was fleeing from Helena.

I suddenly felt an overwhelming weariness. The sort of weariness when everything makes a person indifferent and the only satisfactory form of existence seems resting in his own bed with some illustrated magazines in his hand. I knew this state would rapidly pass and nightmares would immediately follow. I went in the direction of the Market Place.

I saw before me my own absolutely ruined life. Maybe my own fault. Maybe because I'd set myself standards too high for our times. However, since I'd decided on them, I had to make a report of the results. I was glad to remember that I still had a half bottle of brandy at home, genuine Martell. Make a report? But how? In the meantime, let's drink the brandy, and then we'll see.

I entered the Market Place, crossed to the right by the AB, then further by Szczepanski Street in the direction of the City Park. In Szczepanski Square it seemed to me that someone was creeping up behind me and suddenly I heard the cry:

"Hands up!"

I turned around. Behind me was Dorota, index finger outstretched, as though it were a revolver.

"Pop-pop-pop, pop-pop-pop, but brother, I tell you, this is a movie! Bang, bang! Pop-pop-pop! All the enemies lie in the dust in the street. *Vera Cruz*! You never saw anything like it in your life! Bang! Pop-pop-pop! Bang! Pop-pop-pop! Bang! I'll walk with you again, do you want to? Pop-pop-pop! Bang!"

"Fine, of course, but put that Colt away, people are gathering."

People were looking around at us and two guys stopped.

"You couldn't be a cowboy. A few wretched passersby alarm you. If you want, I'll straighten them out and disarm them. Want me to?"

"Forgive them this time."

"Well, only because you ask me to. Are you going home? I can accompany you."

This time I was glad she wanted to accompany me. I was afraid of solitude.

"Know what," I said, "drop by at my place. I have some brandy, we'll get something to eat."

"How should I know? I'll come with you, surely. But drop by? Today I wanted to finish my book."

"That *Peter Pan*?"

"Well? Why are you grinning, stupid? It's a very wise book."

"I'm not laughing at all, only smiling. You can read it at my place. I don't want to be alone today."

"In that case, OK. You didn't have too good a time at that concert. I told you so! You should have come to *Vera Cruz* with me."

She came to my place. And I really don't know how it happened. We ate supper, drank three brandies each, after supper Dorota sat down on the couch and started reading. I lay down and leaned my head on her knees. Not for a moment did I suppose that something might come of this. Lost in reading, she started instinctively to stroke my hair. But how it all happened afterwards, I really don't know.

Dorota closed her book with a bang. I was just dropping off, some strange, colored things were running through my head. I started up.

"What happened?"

"A calf in a bowler hat was dancing on the lawn. I finished the book. Now I'll be off. It'll be dawn soon."

"Wait a little, you were going to tell me about it."

"Oh yes. OK. I'll tell you, then I'll go. So this is how it was: "Children were once birds and they lived in a big park on Bird Island. People who wanted children wrote a letter to the raven Solomon, expressing their wishes, and the raven Solomon sent them a little bird which on the way changed into a little boy or girl. This was how Peter Pan obtained parents. He lay in a cradle with feather bedding, his parents and relatives admired, caressed, and amused him. It was nice, warm, and cosy. But when evening came and the tall, dark shadows of trees on Bird Island were outlined outside the window, uneasiness and longing overcame him. One time he overheard his parents wondering what he'd become when he grew up. The thought that at some time he'd become a grownup, that he'd wear stiff clothes which would constrain his body, spectacles, and whiskers like his father, that he'd walk around with a cane and a briefcase, that like his father he'd carry out numerous funny, useless acts and utter thousands of meaningless and pointless phrases, horrified him so much that he decided to run away and go back to Bird Island, so as never to grow up. One summer evening, when his parents had gone out of the room leaving a window open, Peter Pan flew back to his bird homeland. He didn't realize he was no longer a bird, that he had no feathers or wings and because of that he could still flutter. But when he arrived at the Island, the birds fled from him. Not understanding this, he kept behaving in bird fashion, and after a series of similar experiences he was forced to understand that he wasn't a bird any longer and had nothing in common with birds. Worried, he went for advice to the raven Solomon, but the raven Solomon folded his wings helplessly. Neither he nor anyone else was in a position to change the fact that Peter had stopped being a bird. What was worse, having fled from people, he also stopped being a person, properly speaking. But return was impossible too, for having lost his belief in being a bird, he wouldn't be able to fly any more. Besides, he wouldn't be accepted there either. Immediately after his disappearance, his parents sent an order for another child and it was already occupying Peter's place. There's no help for it, he must remain what he is. But what is he? A bird? No. A person? Not that either. The raven Solomon pondered deeply and finally decided: 'You're neither fish, nor fowl, nor good red herring.'

"And Peter Pan stayed on Bird Island as 'neither fish nor fowl.' He helped the birds build nests, helped the raven Solomon sort orders for children, played on a pipe which he made for himself from a willow for the elves to dance to.

"He was neither happy nor unhappy. And only sometimes on a summer evening, when the noise of the town, the roar of traffic and the clang of streetcar bells came with particular clarity from the direction of the distant park gates, and when the dark outlines of houses and the street lamps sparkled through the trees, a yearning oppressed his heart which he didn't understand."

She recited this in one breath, fluently, as though she'd learned it by heart and somehow so nicely that it shocked me.

"You told that very nicely."

"Well, sure. Why not? You regard me as an idiot, but I have literary gifts. You consider this book stupid, but you're the one who's stupid and the book is wise, wiser than all the articles in the magazines which Agnieszka reads."

"Really?"

"Really. You're precisely 'neither fish nor fowl.' "

"Me?"

"Yes, you. Me too. All of us, in general. I even told that to the trainer. If you only knew! I said, 'Sir, you're neither fish nor fowl.' And he said, 'Dorota, have you gone crazy?' And I said, 'I haven't gone crazy. You're neither fish nor fowl and all of us are neither fish nor fowl.' "

"You're kidding."

"No, I'm not."

"How could you tell him, seeing you've only just finished reading the book at this moment?"

"Brother, I've read it God knows how many times."

"Is that why you had to finish it in order to tell me?"

"There must be some sort of order."

"You're either a genius or a complete idiot."

"Exactly! The trainer once said exactly the same thing to me."

"The trainer. Stop harping on trainer. Can't you say Ksiezak? Even in bed you'd say 'Sir' to him."

"If you only knew!"

"What?"

"Well, just that."

"Dorota, surely I've misunderstood you."

"You understood me very well. In bed I said 'Sir' to him. Well, somehow I've got used to it, so that I can't speak to him any other way. He got mad at it too. He said, 'Call me Edward. On the grounds it is something else, but here you can call me Edward.' However, I couldn't. I got so used to it that I could only say 'Sir.' "

"When was this?"

"Then. In Bucharest. When I twisted my leg and they thought it was a break. When the trainer stayed with me and we came back a day later than you. He was very good to me. Really very good."

"I don't doubt it."

"And do you know what he said? He said that . . ."

"Wait, wait a moment. I must collect my thoughts."

I wanted to collect my thoughts, but it was impossible.

Dorota turned out the lamp. The dawn was breaking through the curtains.

"I'm going now," she said and started to get up. "Thanks for the supper."

It seemed to me that it was all a dream. I mistily saw Dorota dressing and around her danced Peter Pan, playing his pipe, and varicolored little spirits. Why did that have to be a dream vision? After all this, why did just that have to be improbable?

I no longer saw anything, I only felt Dorota cover me thoughtfully with the quilt and then I heard her go out on tiptoe.

"I always had a presentiment you'd commit some folly, I always feared that," said Agnieszka.

Through the barred window the Kosciusko Mound could be seen against the background of sky, a particularly rich blue on that sunny autumn day. It was late afternoon and the sky was slowly growing dark.

We weren't looking at each other. We were both looking at the window.

"You're an enormously unbalanced person," added Agnieszka after a while.

I wanted to reply to this, but she anticipated me:

"Excuse me . . . I'm talking without sense. Don't be mad. Actually I'm thrown off my balance by all this. Surely you understand. By the place and the circumstances. I wanted to see you. Well, after all, you see, since I came. I had to come and see you, but now I don't know how to begin and so I'm somehow talking stupidly."

"If what I did can be called a folly, I committed it for your sake . . . or on your account . . . or however you may call it in the end."

"I know. I know, and I have pangs of conscience. Well, you see I came. I had to come and see you. I have pangs of conscience but I couldn't say for sure that I feel guilty. Pangs of conscience and a feeling of guilt are two different matters. Obviously I ought to have told you about everything earlier. But, believe me, I kept figuring that it would somehow work out, that it would change. Oh, I placed so much faith in you."

"What is it you should have told me about earlier?"

She turned her head from the window and looked at me. I went on looking at the window, at the sky beyond, which was continually darkening.

"Is it essential to speak directly and aloud about that which we both know anyway?"

"As you think fit."

"I do think it's essential. It's necessary to dot the i. But it's so hard and difficult."

She was gazing at me all the time. I stroked my forehead, nose,

eyes, as though I wanted to erase her look from my face. Finally
she lowered her head, opened her bag and took out a handkerchief. I thought she was crying or was going to begin crying, but
she didn't dream of it. She blew her nose. She did it in the way
that women convinced of their culture and elegance do: delicately, silently. For me this manner of blowing the nose is something rather disgusting. She put the handkerchief back in her bag,
and closed the bag so loudly that I jumped. Then she put a finger
on the clasp, parted her lips and started looking at the window
again. Objectively speaking, she looked pretty and interesting,
but she couldn't please me. I was mad that she'd come. I had an
enormous desire to throw her out of the window and the irrelevant thought came into my head that I wouldn't be able to, on account of the bars. Why did this thought come into my head? In
any case, I wouldn't have thrown her out.

The silence lasted a very long time, but I hadn't the slightest intention of persuading her to hold forth.

In the lobby of the "Phoenix," right by the cloakroom, three
men were holding me forcefully, although I wasn't struggling nor
did I betray any such intentions. I had a split lip and a swollen
face. My leg hurt where the smallest of the three men, with a pink
round mug, kicked me. I thought to myself that assuredly St.
Stanislas Kostka, whom I personally never liked as a saint and
whom I suspected of deceit, looked like that. The others were
twisting my arms while he, St. Stanislas Kostka, was holding me
by the lapels. He thrust his face close to mine and insulted me
quietly, passionately, with skill. I bore it some time patiently,
until with a light movement of the head I banged him hard. I
didn't do this out of rage, because there wasn't any rage in me,
but out of boredom. Time was dragging for me until the police arrived. St. Stanislas Kostka howled, grabbed his nose and right
away all three again began hitting me. This lasted a short time,
because just then the nervous wail of a siren resounded and after
a moment two policemen came in, with helmet straps under their
chins. They walked slowly, but when the others caught sight of
them, they stopped hitting me and let go. I took out a handkerchief and wiped my nose. The people watching all this, who had
been curious at first and even excited, now looked weary and
overcome with distaste. They began withdrawing in silence, and
the cloakroom attendant burst out with an idiotic laugh, but he
broke off abruptly and gazed with open mouth at the approaching policemen.

"Good evening, all," said the sergeant, "I'm happy you're enjoying yourselves."

The other policeman, without a badge of rank, was picking his teeth with a toothpick and gazing fixedly to one side; it seemed as though none of this concerned him.

"Sergeant," said the man who had twisted my left arm, and whom I'd previously punched on the jaw. "He intended to kill a woman, and when we went to her defense he wanted to fight us."

"Meanwhile," replied the sergeant, "I see that you've been hitting him."

"But, sergeant," cried the man who had twisted my right arm and whom I'd previously struck in the stomach, that he'd curled up into a ball and flown onto the table at which a fat man with smoothly licked hair and as many as four women of various ages were sitting. The table overturned, the fat man lay on the floor and the women screamed.

"They're telling the truth," I said, "I did want to kill this woman."

The sergeant glanced at me coldly.

"Meanwhile I haven't asked you about anything," he said slowly and loudly, but not in a raised voice.

I shrugged and St. Stanislas Kostka cried:

"Yes, he wanted to kill her. She was standing quietly at the bar drinking orange juice, and he threw himself at her for no reason whatsoever and shouted he would kill her and he called her names and grabbed her by the shoulders and started banging her head on the top of the bar, and when we rushed to help her he manhandled us, before we managed to overpower him. He said he's Arens, but he can't be *the* Arens, can he? We searched his pockets, but he hasn't any papers. Sergeant, you surely know Arens well. Can he be Arens? He struck me in the nose with his head with all his might. He's broken my nose, for sure."

The sergeant cast a glance at me, barely surveyed me and said:

"No, this isn't Arens. We'll clear up who he is, never fear."

"I said so from the start," cried the guy who'd got it in the stomach. "Arens ought to bring the law against him too. We'll bear witness."

"Sure," said the sergeant, "you'll bear witness and you'll explain what entitled you to substitute for the police and search this man."

The three glanced at one another helplessly until at last St. Stanislas Kostka said quietly:

"He wanted to kill a woman, and he broke my nose."

"We'll confirm how it all was in reality. Meanwhile, I'll ask you citizens for your identity papers. Where's the alleged victim?"

"Not alleged. She has a really and truly cracked head and is at the first-aid station," said the guy who'd got it on the jaw. He said it with a very sweet and completely inappropriate smile, considering the time.

The policeman with the toothpick took their papers from them and began copying down details.

I felt rather sorry for these three. Maybe they were peaceable and honest citizens who'd come to have a good time and acted in good faith, but I'd drawn them into such a stupid brawl.

"We acted in self-defense," cried St. Stanislas Kostka desperately.

"In the first place, in defense of the attacked woman," the guy who'd got it on the jaw said with dignity. "She's at the first-aid station."

"I heard that already," stated the sergeant drily. "We'll find out how it all happened and I can promise you gentlemen we shan't make any mistakes. I advise you all the same never again to intrude on the powers of the police. You can all go home. You'll be summoned when the need arises. And in general please break it up," he shouted, and looked around angrily.

Those who still felt like staying shivered and began going down the stairs backward.

"Let's go," said the sergeant to me, "will you go quietly or do I have to put handcuffs on you?"

"I'll be crazy and bite," I said, but he shrugged and shoved me lightly.

We started going downstairs. In the car we were silent for some time. The sergeant was sitting beside me in the back, the policeman with the toothpick at the wheel. The sergeant was whistling through his teeth and suddenly said:

"What have you been up to?"

"Nothing. I wanted to kill this woman."

"Stop making a fool of yourself. What really happened there in the 'Phoenix'?"

"Do I have to tell you?"

"As you wish. In any case I'll get you out of it."

"I'm not asking you to."

"I also didn't ask you for anything when we were fighting in the ring and you didn't knock me out, though you could have. Tell me, what's happening to you? After all, it's clear that such a brawl didn't arise through your fault."

"What makes you so sure that it's clear?"

"Because I know you. This isn't in your line."

"Everyone sooner or later must do something that isn't in his line, and others are surprised. This is because nobody has any line, everyone only pretends."

"You had me on the hook. You could have knocked me out and you let me last to the finish. Was that too some sort of pretense?"

"I don't recall. Maybe. We were seventeen at the time."

"But I recall. You knew that a girl who mattered to me was sitting in the audience.

"You're boring and sentimental."

"That was your line. But after all it isn't only from that that I know you. I'll pull you out of this mess even if it *was* all your fault. I know you, and everybody knows you."

"Nobody knows me. Nonsense. Where are we going?"

"How come 'where'? Home. Skowronski, make a turn. Drive to Slowacki Boulevard. Do you still live there?"

"You'll take me to the station, Kosmala."

"Don't make a fool of yourself. And don't worry about a thing. Who was she, that woman?"

"Lola 'Fiat 1100.' "

Sergeant Kosmala whistled.

"The one Szymaniak killed himself for?"

"The same."

"Did you really want to kill her?"

"Really."

"Why?"

"I thought it would settle everything."

"What everything? Revenge for Szymaniak? So long after?"

"That too. But not only that. In general everything."

"I don't understand."

"You don't have to understand."

"And if those three hadn't prevented you, you'd have killed her?"

"They didn't prevent me. I didn't know how to kill her. I didn't know how it's done. Yet again in my life I've made a fool of myself. I'm 'neither fish nor fowl.' And you're 'neither fish nor fowl.' We're all 'neither fish nor fowl.' "

"All right, all right. We're 'neither fish nor fowl.' It can happen to everyone, just as it can happen to anyone that he hits the gas and makes a bit of a mess. Sleep it off and you'll forget it all. We'll forget too, eh, Skowronski?"

"Of course," said Skowronski and he swore, because the toothpick flew out of his mouth.

"Those jokers of witnesses needn't be feared. I deliberately scared them. They'll be glad when they realize that nobody is concerned with them any more. As for Lola 'Fiat 1100,' I take the responsibility. Even if she recognized you, I have arguments that will quiet her."

"You're wearing me out, Kosmala. Stop chattering and let's go to the station."

"You'll sleep it off and everything will be all right. And don't fear that I'll have troubles on your account. There's no one who'd want to give you a bad name on account of one stupid scrap after drinking. Especially now, before the Memorial. Is it true you'll be running in the five thousand?"

"Kosmala, get into your head what I'm saying to you: don't treat me as a drunk and do what I ask. After all, we're grownup men. When we were both seventeen we fought together, we knew how to respect one another and already then we were men. Then! But today! Today I'm mostly surrounded by such soft, commonplace types who, though they're past the thirty mark, aren't yet men and assuredly never will be. And I'm scared that among them I myself am changing into just such a commonplace nothing, but I don't want to and I'm defending myself against it as best I can and know how. Listen, I'll tell you: You consider that once I could knock you out but I didn't do so, because a girl whom you loved was sitting in the audience. It wasn't at all like that. I didn't knock you out so that *I* could please her, to show her what I could afford and how generous I was. And later, on that account, I slept with her. So you see? Man, I wanted to be noble and just in this life, I wanted to keep my word, not betray anyone or cheat anyone and somehow it never worked out. There's no law which would punish someone for wanting to do good in life, though it worked out badly for him, and no law can punish me for a particular injustice which I did to a certain person. I want to start life again and I want it to be the life of a man who's ruthlessly honest. But before that I must obliterate everything that has been up till now. But since no court can pass a sentence on me for cheating and betraying a girl to whom I made a vow, and what a vow, let it sentence me for something else. What's the difference? I see you don't understand me, and I don't know how to make it clearer to you. And I don't know how to explain to you why I behave this way and not some other way. Maybe because I read the

novel *Resurrection* and that Nekhljudov impressed me like few others. Maybe on account of pride and haughtiness that I don't want
to accept the norms of life which people living around me have established and which I consider hypocritical and false. Or maybe
simply because when performing a somersault in my childhood I
fell on my head. Listen, Kosmala, let's drive to the police station
and stop making fools of ourselves."

Sergeant Kosmala listened to me attentively, his head buried in
his hands, and with his forehead wrinkled. When I finished he
seemed to debate with himself for a while and great uneasiness
and effort showed on his face. Finally he straightened up and said
to the driver:

"Turn around, Skowronski. We'll go to the station."

And he at once turned to me:

"Don't be a swine and don't think it's on account of that girl.
Anyway, I don't believe this nonsense. You made it up. You're
better, wiser, and more educated than I am, and I have to respect
what you wish even though it seems stupid to me."

Agnieszka opened her bag again, brought out her handkerchief
and blew her nose again in the same way.

"You've got a cold," I said.

She sighed.

"So is it essential to talk about it all?"

"You think so, not I."

I felt weary and longed for her to go.

"Yes. I think so. I put off telling you the truth for a long time. If
that can be a justification, I also put off telling it to myself. I don't
love you, Marek, and I never loved you. Am I doing right in telling you this just now? I'm certain it's right. After all, you can explain everything to yourself during this year. Wouldn't it be worse
for you if you were to come out of jail hoping I'd be waiting for
you and maybe something could go on between us? True, that
would be worse, wouldn't it?"

I bowed my head low and nodded. I didn't want her to know
how I was struggling to prevent a burst of laughter. Sincere, frank
laughter.

"It's good that you agree with this. We knew it would be best
for you this way. We decided together. You know . . . Michal
and I . . . We're getting married . . . this has been going on a
long time already between us. I don't want you to think that it all
came easily to me, that it was so simple. You really meant something to me and in a certain way you still do. Our meeting oc-

curred at a special moment. I'd lived through a series of disappointments and disillusionments and it seemed to me that it was enough in life to sacrifice oneself for someone who needs us in order to gain tranquillity and self-respect. And at first I experienced this. I experienced this though it tortured me to pretend to be the kind of woman you needed and who could please you. Because basically I'm entirely different and you don't really know me. I wanted to make a man of you and I was happy when I saw I had some influence over you and that you were changing, but then came the disastrous moment when I understood that it was a mistake and that nothing in life can be done by force. Then I met Michal, you introduced me to him, and everything got muddled up. I felt that it ought to be explained as soon as possible, but I continually lacked the courage because I realized with despair that I was essential to you, that you couldn't live without me and that you wouldn't stop loving me so easily. I also saw that you felt something wasn't in order between us and that you were suffering terribly for fear of losing me. I kept making up my mind to talk to you finally and to confess everything. And I kept drawing back, trembling at your suffering which I myself was causing you. On the day of the concert, I spent the entire day with Michal. We talked about all this, about the necessity of a final decision of matters between us. You don't even know how Michal is attached to you. It was hard for him too. It was and is. After the concert we met again and decided we must not put it off any longer, that immediately, right away, I must meet you and face that which had to be admitted. I decided to go after you to Artur's, bring you away from him and talk finally. When I entered his gateway I shone my flashlight and saw you leaning against a pillar. You were standing motionless, plunged in thought. Was it hard for me to guess what thoughts they were? I called to you quietly, but you didn't even stir. And then, yet again, I took fright and withdrew. My panicky fear declined before the enormity of your feelings and my inability to fulfill them. I switched off the flashlight and ran away. Why, why? Maybe I'd have succeeded in convincing you, explaining everything and you wouldn't have committed out of desperation the insane things that have brought you to this point . . . Listen, I'm going now. Better that I went. Tell . . ."

"Go, Agnieszka."

Facing me there was a year in jail and then hellish difficulty over a newly started life which was to be the life of an absolutely honest man. I already knew it wouldn't be. Integrity can only have meaning when it is collective property. When someone wants to appropriate it alone, it makes a victim of him. Not only deserving of pity, but also comic.

So have I lost everything? No! Jowita is left to me. I never stopped thinking about Jowita. She was the one bright and pure happening in my life. Thanks to her I even knew how to endure imprisonment. I would stand at the bars, gaze at the Kosciuszko Mound, think of her and carry on long conversations with her about everything that had happened and also about what hadn't happened but that might have happened. I knew now what was beyond the Mound. Beyond the Mound are the antipodes, and Jowita lives in the antipodes. The antipodes are distant, very distant. But what significance has that? She was, she existed.

The warden opened the door for Agnieszka. She hesitated again, turned back for a moment and said:

"This is of course a trivial and meaningless matter at this time, but in the last analysis it all started from this, so surely I ought to tell you: I was Jowita."

The autumn afternoon was going rapidly to meet the evening, the sky beyond the barred window was turning pink in the sunset. The outline of the Kosciuszko Mound darkened, the key grated in the door beyond which Agnieszka had disappeared.

"O my unhappy mother! O my accursed donkey's ears!"